D1498533

Keep it Simple. Make it Special.

Cook it Quick

Dedication

For every busy cook, whether new to the kitchen or experienced, who wants a home-cooked meal in a jiffy!

Appreciation

Thanks to everyone who shared their very favorite quick & easy recipes with us!

Gooseberry Patch
An imprint of Globe Pequot
246 Goose Lane • Guilford, CT 06437

www.gooseberrypatch.com
1•800•854•6673

Copyright 2015, Gooseberry Patch 978-1-62093-214-8
First Printing, 2016

All rights reserved. No part of this book may be reproduced or utilized in any form or by any means, electronic or mechanical, including photocopying and recording, or by any information storage and retrieval system, without permission in writing from the publisher. Printed in Korea.

Table of Contents

U.S. to Metric Recipe Equivalents

Volume Measurements

1/4 teaspoon	1 mL
1/2 teaspoon	2 mL
1 teaspoon	5 mL
1 tablespoon = 3 teaspoons	15 mL
2 tablespoons = 1 fluid ounce	30 mL
1/4 cup	60 mL
1/3 cup	75 mL
1/2 cup = 4 fluid ounces	125 mL
1 cup = 8 fluid ounces	250 mL
2 cups = 1 pint =16 fluid ounces	500 mL
4 cups = 1 quart	1 L

Weights

1 ounce	30 g
4 ounces	120 g
8 ounces	225 g
16 ounces = 1 pound	450 g

Oven Temperatures

300° F	150° C
325° F	160° C
350° F	180° C
375° F	190° C
400° F	200° C
450° F	230° C

Baking Pan Sizes

Square

8x8x2 inches	2 L = 20x20x5 cm
9x9x2 inches	2.5 L = 23x23x5 cm

Rectangular

13x9x2 inches	3.5 L = 33x23x5 cm

Loaf

9x5x3 inches	2 L = 23x13x7 cm

Round

8x1-1/2 inches	1.2 L = 20x4 cm
9x1-1/2 inches	1.5 L = 23x4 cm

Recipe Abbreviations

t. = teaspoon	ltr. = liter
T. = tablespoon	oz. = ounce
c. = cup	lb. = pound
pt. = pint	doz. = dozen
qt. = quart	pkg. = package
gal. = gallon	env. = envelope

Kitchen Measurements

A pinch = 1/8 tablespoon	1 fluid ounce = 2 tablespoons
3 teaspoons = 1 tablespoon	4 fluid ounces = 1/2 cup
2 tablespoons = 1/8 cup	8 fluid ounces = 1 cup
4 tablespoons = 1/4 cup	16 fluid ounces = 1 pint
8 tablespoons = 1/2 cup	32 fluid ounces = 1 quart
16 tablespoons = 1 cup	16 ounces net weight = 1 pound
2 cups = 1 pint	
4 cups = 1 quart	
4 quarts = 1 gallon	

Pepperoni Puffs

Pepperoni Puffs

Marcia Marcoux, Charlton, MA

1 c. all-purpose flour
1 t. baking powder
1 c. milk
1 egg, beaten

1 c. shredded Cheddar
  cheese
1-1/2 c. pepperoni, diced

Combine flour, baking powder, milk, egg and cheese; mix well. Stir in pepperoni; let stand for 15 minutes. Spoon into greased mini muffin cups, filling 3/4 full. Bake at 350 degrees for 25 to 35 minutes, until golden. Makes 2 dozen.

BBQ Nachos Deluxe

Donna Roe, Merrimack, NH

1-1/2 lbs. ground beef
16-oz. can refried beans
18-oz. bottle barbecue
  sauce
20-oz. pkg. tortilla chips

2-1/4 oz. can sliced black
  olives, drained
2 8-oz. pkgs. shredded
  Mexican-blend cheese
Garnish: sour cream

Brown beef in a skillet over medium heat; drain. Stir in beans and barbecue sauce. Simmer until heated through, about 5 minutes. Spread tortilla chips evenly on an ungreased baking sheet. Spoon beef mixture evenly over chips. Sprinkle olives and cheese on top. Bake at 350 degrees for 15 to 18 minutes. Garnish with sour cream. Makes 4 to 6 servings.

Pizza Fondue

Michelle Golz, Freeport, IL

1 lb. ground beef
1 onion, chopped
2 10-oz. cans pizza sauce
1 T. cornstarch
1-1/2 t. fennel seed
1-1/2 t. dried oregano
1/4 t. garlic powder

2-1/2 c. shredded Cheddar
  cheese
2 c. shredded
  mozzarella cheese
2 loaves French bread,
  sliced and toasted

Brown ground beef and onion in a skillet over medium heat; drain. Add remaining ingredients except bread; simmer until cheese melts. Serve hot with bread slices for dipping. Serves 6 to 8.

Quick tip

Arrange nachos on a large oven-proof serving tray before popping them into the oven...one less pan to wash after the party!

Julie's Fresh Guacamole

Julie Dos Santos, Fort Pierce, FL

6 avocados, halved and pitted
3 T. lime juice
1/2 yellow onion, finely chopped
4 roma tomatoes, chopped
3/4 c. sour cream

1 T. ranch salad
  dressing
1 T. salt, or to taste
1 T. pepper, or to taste
1 T. chili powder

1/2 t. cayenne pepper
Garnish: fresh cilantro sprigs
tortilla chips

Scoop out avocado pulp into a large bowl; mash with a fork. Add lime juice, onion and tomatoes; mix with a spoon. Add sour cream, salad dressing and seasonings; mix well. Cover with plastic wrap; refrigerate for at least 30 minutes. Garnish with cilantro. Serve with tortilla chips. Makes 8 to 10 servings.

Homemade Tortilla Chips

Megan Brooks, Antioch, TN

6 corn tortillas, each cut into
  8 wedges

kosher salt to taste

Spread tortilla wedges on an ungreased baking sheet in a single layer. Bake at 350 degrees for 8 to 10 minutes, until crisp. While still warm, spray each chip lightly with non-stick vegetable spray. Sprinkle salt lightly over both sides of chips. Makes 4 dozen.

Julie's Fresh Guacamole

Creamy BLT Dip

Jalapeño Cheese Spread

Kerri Cordova, Martinez, CA

2 8-oz. pkgs. cream
   cheese, softened
1 t. lemon juice
3 to 4 roasted jalapeño
   peppers, seeded and
   chopped

2-oz. jar diced
   pimentos, drained
1 T. mayonnaise
1/8 t. salt
assorted crackers
   or tortillas

Combine all ingredients except crackers or tortillas.
Mix well. Cover and refrigerate overnight. Serve with
crackers or spread on warmed tortillas. Makes about
2 cups.

Creamy BLT Dip

Barbara Thurman, Carlyle, IL

1 lb. bacon, crisply cooked
   and crumbled
1 c. mayonnaise
1 c. sour cream

2 tomatoes, chopped
Optional: chopped fresh
   chives

Blend together bacon, mayonnaise and sour cream;
chill. Stir in tomatoes just before serving; sprinkle
with chives, if desired. Makes 2-1/2 cups.

Greek Spread

Stephanie Doyle, Lincoln University, PA

1 c. plus 1 T. chopped
   almonds, divided
8-oz. pkg. crumbled feta
   cheese
7-oz. jar roasted red
   peppers, drained and
   chopped

1 clove garlic, chopped
2 8-oz. pkgs. cream
   cheese, softened
10-oz. pkg. frozen spinach,
   thawed and drained
crackers or pita wedges

Line a 2-quart bowl with plastic wrap; sprinkle in one
tablespoon almonds. In a separate bowl, mix together
1/2 cup almonds, feta cheese, peppers, garlic, cream
cheese and spinach; blend well. Press into bowl over
almonds. Cover and chill overnight. Invert onto a serving
dish. Remove plastic wrap; press remaining almonds
onto the outside. Serve with crackers or pita wedges.
Makes about 7 cups.

Quick tip

A table runner really dresses up a
table, and you can make one in no
time at all. Just stitch together several
vintage-style tea towels, end-to-end.

Toasted Ravioli

Diane Cohen, The Woodlands, TX

9-oz. pkg. refrigerated
  cheese-filled ravioli
1/2 c. Italian-flavored seasoned
  dry bread crumbs

1/4 c. milk
1 egg

Garnish: grated Parmesan cheese,
  warm spaghetti sauce

Cook ravioli in boiling water for 3 minutes. Drain well and cool slightly. Place bread crumbs in a shallow dish. In another shallow dish, beat together milk and egg. Dip ravioli in egg mixture and let excess drip off. Dip in bread crumbs to coat. Place ravioli on a lightly greased baking sheet. Bake at 425 degrees for 15 minutes, or until crisp and golden. Sprinkle ravioli with Parmesan cheese and serve with warm spaghetti sauce. Makes 8 to 10 servings.

Smokey Sausage Wraps

Vickie McMonigal, Altoona, PA

16-oz. pkg. cheese-filled
  cocktail sausages
3 T. barbecue sauce

1 T. maple syrup
8-oz. tube refrigerated
  crescent rolls

Garnish: additional barbecue
  sauce

Place 32 sausages in a medium saucepan; reserve any remaining sausages for another recipe. Stir in barbecue sauce and maple syrup. Cook over medium heat until heated through; let cool for 5 to 10 minutes. Separate crescents into triangles; cut each triangle into 4 long, thin triangles. Wrap one triangle of dough around each sausage; pinch ends to seal. Arrange on an ungreased baking sheet. Bake at 350 degrees until golden. Serve with additional sauce for dipping. Makes 32 wraps.

Toasted Ravioli

🥄🍴🔪 *Quick side*

For a quick & easy snack that everybody loves, nothing beats a big bowl of fresh-popped popcorn! To add new flavor, sprinkle on grated Parmesan cheese, taco seasoning mix or cinnamon-sugar.

Cheese Pops

Fried Dill Pickles
Tina George, El Dorado, AR

3 eggs
1 c. milk
1 c. Italian-seasoned dry bread crumbs
1/4 c. all-purpose flour
15 dill pickle spears, well drained
oil for deep frying
Garnish: ranch or Thousand Island salad dressing

Whisk together eggs and milk in a small bowl; mix bread crumbs and flour in a separate small bowl. Dip pickles into egg mixture; roll in crumb mixture to coat. Heat several inches oil to 375 degrees in a deep fryer. Fry pickles, 3 to 5 at a time, until golden. Drain on paper towels. Serve warm with salad dressing for dipping. Makes 4 to 5 servings.

Cheese Pops
Carol Hickman, Kingsport, TN

2 3-oz. pkgs. cream cheese, softened
2 c. finely shredded Cheddar cheese
2 t. honey
1-1/2 c. carrots, peeled and finely shredded
1 c. pecans, finely chopped
4 doz. pretzel sticks

Combine cheeses, honey and carrots; chill for one hour. Shape into one-inch balls and then roll in pecans. Chill, then insert pretzel sticks before serving. Makes 3 to 4 dozen.

Mushroom Poppers
Julianne Saifullah, Lexington, KY

16 mushrooms
2 cloves garlic, minced
2 jalapeño peppers, finely chopped, ribs and seeds removed
1 T. olive oil
2 3-oz. pkgs. cream cheese, softened
1/4 c. plus 2 T. shredded Cheddar cheese
4 slices bacon, crisply cooked and crumbled
salt and pepper to taste

Separate mushroom stems from caps; set caps aside. Finely chop stems. In a skillet over medium heat, cook chopped stems, garlic and peppers in oil; cook and stir until mushrooms are tender, about 10 minutes. Transfer mushroom mixture to a bowl; stir in cheeses and bacon. Season with salt and pepper. Spoon mushroom mixture generously into reserved mushroom caps; arrange caps in a lightly greased 13"x9" baking pan. Bake, uncovered, at 350 degrees for 15 to 20 minutes, until golden on top. Serves 8.

Maple Chicken Wings

Donna Nowicki, Center City, MN

2 to 3 lbs. chicken wings
1 c. maple syrup
2/3 c. chili sauce

1/2 c. onion, finely chopped
2 T. Dijon mustard
2 t. Worcestershire sauce

1/4 to 1/2 t. red pepper flakes

Place wings in a large plastic zipping bag; set aside. Combine remaining ingredients. Reserve one cup for basting; refrigerate until ready to use. Pour remaining marinade over wings, turning to coat. Seal bag; refrigerate for 4 hours, turning occasionally. Drain and discard marinade. Place wings in a lightly greased 13"x9" baking pan. Bake, uncovered, at 375 degrees for 30 to 40 minutes, basting with reserved marinade, until golden and juices run clear when pierced. Makes 2 to 3 dozen.

Maple-Topped Sweet Potato Skins

Linda Corcoran, Metuchen, NJ

6 sweet potatoes
1/2 c. cream cheese, softened
1/4 c. sour cream
2 t. cinnamon, divided

2 t. nutmeg, divided
2 t. ground ginger, divided
2 c. chopped walnuts or pecans
3 T. butter, softened

1/4 c. brown sugar, packed
Garnish: warm maple syrup,
  additional nuts

Pierce potatoes with a fork. Bake at 400 degrees or microwave on high setting until tender; cool. Slice each potato in half lengthwise; scoop out baked insides, keeping skins intact. Place potato skins on an ungreased baking sheet. Mash baked potato in a bowl until smooth; add cream cheese, sour cream and one teaspoon each of spices. Mix well and spoon into potato skins. In a bowl, mix nuts, butter, brown sugar and remaining spices; sprinkle over top. Bake at 400 degrees for 15 minutes. Drizzle with warm maple syrup; garnish as desired. Makes one dozen.

Maple-Topped Sweet Potato Skins

Quick tip

Show your hometown spirit...cheer on the high school football team with a neighborhood block party. Invite neighbors to bring along their favorite appetizers to share and don't forget to wear school colors!

Quick tip

Appetizer spreads are perfect for enjoying during card games or a favorite movie at home with friends! Set out a variety of creamy dips, crunchy snacks and sweet munchies along with fizzy beverages...then relax and enjoy your guests.

Jalapeño Poppers

Jalapeño Poppers

Sue Bodner, New York, NY

24 pickled jalapeño peppers
1 lb. Cheddar cheese
1/2 c. cornmeal

1/2 c. all-purpose flour
1 t. salt
2 eggs, beaten

oil for deep frying

Make a short slit into each jalapeño pepper; remove as many seeds as possible. Slice cheese into strips 1/4" wide and one-inch long; insert one in each jalapeño. Combine cornmeal, flour and salt in a small bowl; place beaten eggs in a separate bowl. Dip peppers into egg mixture; roll in cornmeal mixture until well coated. Set aside on a wire rack for 30 minutes. Add 4 inches of oil to a deep fryer; heat to about 375 degrees. Add poppers in small batches; cook until crisp and golden, about 4 minutes. Remove poppers using a slotted spoon; drain on paper towels. Makes 2 dozen.

Chicky Popovers

Deanna Lyons, Columbus, OH

8-oz. pkg. cream cheese, softened
3 boneless, skinless chicken
  breasts, cooked and shredded
1-1/2 t. sesame seed
1/4 t. dried parsley

1 T. onion, minced
1 t. garlic, minced
1/2 c. spinach, finely chopped
Optional: 1/2 c. mushrooms, finely
  chopped

salt and pepper to taste
2 8-oz. tubes refrigerated crescent
  rolls

In a medium bowl, combine all ingredients except crescent rolls; mix well. Open crescent rolls but do not separate into triangles. Instead, pair triangles to form 8 squares. Pinch seams together. Spoon chicken mixture evenly over squares. Fold up corners into center, layering like flower petals so each roll is sealed. Place popovers on a lightly greased baking sheet. Bake at 350 degrees for 12 to 15 minutes, until golden and heated through. Makes 8 servings.

Pull-Apart Pizza Bread

Andy Burton, Dublin, OH

12-oz. tube refrigerated
  flaky biscuits
1 T. olive oil
12 slices pepperoni,
  quartered
1 onion, chopped

1/4 c. shredded
  pizza-blend cheese
1/4 c. grated Parmesan
  cheese
1 t. Italian seasoning
1/4 t. garlic salt

Cut each biscuit into 4 pieces; place in a bowl. Toss biscuit pieces with oil and set aside. In a separate bowl, combine remaining ingredients; mix well. Add biscuits; toss well to coat. Arrange in a Bundt® pan lined with well-greased aluminum foil. Bake at 400 degrees for 15 minutes, or until golden. Turn bread out of pan onto a serving plate while still warm. Makes about 2 dozen pieces.

Firehouse Hot Meatballs

Lea Burwell, Charles Town, WV

40-oz. pkg. frozen
  meatballs
2 15-oz. bottles hot & spicy
  catsup

2-ltr. bottle ginger ale

Place frozen meatballs in a slow cooker; pour both bottles of catsup over top. Add enough ginger ale to cover meatballs. Cover and cook on high setting for one hour. Turn setting to low; cook an additional 3 to 4 hours. Stir before serving. Makes about 6-1/2 dozen.

Buffalo Chicken Salad Sliders

Wendy Perry, Lorton, VA

3/4 c. mayonnaise
1/4 c. sour cream
2 T. hot pepper sauce
1 t. garlic powder
1/2 t. salt

3 c. cooked chicken, diced
3/4 c. celery, diced
1/2 c. sweet onion, diced
8 potato dinner rolls, split

In a bowl, combine mayonnaise, sour cream, hot sauce and seasonings until well mixed. Stir in chicken, celery and onion. Top rolls with chicken mixture. Makes 8.

Buffalo Chicken Salad Sliders

Cranberry & Blue Cheese Ball

Cranberry & Blue Cheese Ball

Kristie Rigo, Friedens, PA

8-oz. pkg. cream cheese, softened
1 c. sharp white Cheddar cheese, shredded
4-oz. container crumbled blue cheese
6-oz. pkg. sweetened dried cranberries
assorted crackers

Place all ingredients except crackers into a food processor; process until well combined. Shape cheese mixture into a ball on a length of plastic wrap; wrap well and refrigerate overnight. Let stand at room temperature for 30 minutes before serving. Serve with assorted crackers. Makes about 3 cups.

Pineapple Cheese Ball

Julie Ann Perkins, Anderson, IN

2 8-oz. pkgs. cream cheese, softened
8-oz. can pineapple tidbits, drained
2 to 4 T. onion, chopped
1/2 c. green pepper, chopped
1/2 t. salt
Optional: pepper to taste
2 c. chopped pecans or walnuts
snack crackers, pita wedges and celery sticks

In a bowl, mix together cream cheese, pineapple, onion, green pepper and seasonings. Roll into one or 2 balls. Roll in chopped nuts to coat. Wrap in plastic wrap; keep refrigerated. Serve with crackers, pita wedges and celery. Serves 10 to 15.

Fresh Fruit Salsa

Ruth Veazey, San Antonio, TX

2 apples, peeled, cored and diced
2 kiwi, peeled and diced
1 c. strawberries, sliced
1/2 c. orange juice
zest of one orange
2 T. brown sugar, packed
2 T. apple jelly
sugar and cinnamon to taste
10-1/2 oz. pkg. flour tortillas, cut into triangles
sugar and cinnamon to taste

Combine apples, kiwi, strawberries, orange juice, zest, brown sugar and apple jelly; cover and refrigerate. Sprinkle sugar and cinnamon over the tortillas; place on an ungreased baking sheet. Bake at 325 degrees until warmed; remove from oven and let cool. Serve with salsa. Makes 5 cups.

Quick tip

Use muffin tins to make giant ice cubes for a party pitcher of lemonade or sweet tea...they'll last much longer than regular ice cubes!

Baja Shrimp Quesadillas

Jo Ann

2-1/2 lbs. shrimp, peeled and cleaned
3 c. shredded Cheddar cheese
1/2 c. mayonnaise
3/4 c. salsa
1/4 t. ground cumin
1/4 t. cayenne pepper
1/4 t. pepper
12 6-inch flour tortillas

Chop shrimp, discarding tails. Mix shrimp, cheese, mayonnaise, salsa, cumin and peppers; spread one to 2 tablespoons on one tortilla. Place another tortilla on top; put on a greased baking sheet. Repeat with remaining tortillas. Bake at 350 degrees for 15 minutes; remove and cut into triangles. Makes about 4 dozen.

Reuben Rolls

Teresa Mulhern, University Heights, OH

12-oz. can corned beef, sliced and shredded
8-oz. pkg. shredded Swiss cheese
2/3 c. sauerkraut, rinsed and drained
1/4 c. sweet onion, finely chopped
15 to 20 egg roll wrappers
oil for deep frying
Garnish: Thousand Island salad dressing

Combine corned beef, cheese, sauerkraut and onion in a bowl. Spoon about 2 tablespoons of mixture into the center of each egg roll wrapper. Fold sides of wrapper in and roll up egg-roll style, sealing edges with water. Heat oil to 350 degrees in a deep saucepan. Deep-fry rolls, a few at a time, until golden on all sides, 3 to 4 minutes. Remove from oil with a slotted spoon; drain on paper towels. Serve warm with salad dressing for dipping. Makes 15 to 20.

Spicy Honey-Molasses Wings

Dema Rankin, Columbus, OH

5 lbs. chicken wings
2-1/2 c. spicy catsup
2/3 c. vinegar
1/2 c. plus 2 T. honey
1/2 c. molasses
1 t. salt
1 t. Worcestershire sauce
1/2 t. onion powder
1/2 t. chili powder
Optional: 1/2 to 1 t. smoke-flavored cooking sauce

Arrange wings in a greased 15"x10" jelly-roll pan. Bake, uncovered, at 375 degrees for 30 minutes. Drain; turn wings and return to oven for an additional 20 to 25 minutes. While wings are baking, combine remaining ingredients in a large saucepan. Bring to a boil; reduce heat and simmer, uncovered, for 25 to 30 minutes. Arrange 1/3 of wings in a large slow cooker; top with one cup sauce. Repeat layers twice. Cover and cook on low setting for 3 to 4 hours; stir gently before serving. Makes about 4 dozen.

Quick side

For an instant appetizer, toss a drained jar of Italian antipasto mix with bite-size cubes of mozzarella cheese. Serve with party picks.

Spicy Honey-Molasses Wings

Vickie's Gazpacho Dip

Vickie's Gazpacho Dip

Vickie

3 tomatoes, diced
3 avocados, pitted, peeled
  and diced
4 green onions, thinly sliced

4-oz. can diced green chiles
3 T. olive oil
1-1/2 T. cider vinegar
1 t. garlic salt

1 t. salt
1/4 t. pepper
tortilla chips

Combine tomatoes, avocados, onions and chiles in a large bowl; set aside. Combine all remaining ingredients except tortilla chips; drizzle over tomato mixture and toss gently. Cover and chill. Serve with chips. Makes about 6 cups.

Cincinnati-Style Chili Dip

Tara Horton, Delaware, OH

8-oz. pkg. cream cheese, softened
10-1/2 oz. can chili without beans

8-oz. pkg. shredded mild Cheddar
  cheese

tortilla chips

Spread cream cheese in an ungreased 8"x8" baking pan. Pour chili over top and sprinkle with cheese. Bake, uncovered, at 350 degrees for 10 to 15 minutes, until cheese is melted. Serve with tortilla chips. Serves 10.

Cheesy Potato Puffs

Barb Sulser, Columbus, OH

4-oz. pkg. instant
  potato flakes
1/2 c. shredded
  Cheddar cheese

1/2 c. bacon bits
Optional: paprika

Prepare potato flakes according to package directions; let cool. Stir in cheese; roll into 1-1/2 inch balls. Roll balls in bacon bits; arrange on an ungreased baking sheet. Sprinkle with paprika, if desired. Bake at 375 degrees for 15 to 18 minutes. Serves 4.

Mozzarella Sticks

Shari Miller, Hobart, IN

2 eggs, beaten
1 T. water
1 c. bread crumbs
2-1/2 t. Italian seasoning
1/2 t. garlic powder

1/8 t. pepper
12 string cheese sticks
3 T. all-purpose flour
1 T. butter, melted

Whisk eggs and water together in a small bowl; set aside. Combine bread crumbs, Italian seasoning, garlic powder and pepper in a plastic zipping bag; set aside. Coat cheese sticks in flour; dip in egg mixture, then shake in bread crumb mixture. Cover; refrigerate for 4 hours. Arrange on an ungreased baking sheet; drizzle with butter. Bake at 400 degrees for 6 to 8 minutes. Let cool for 3 to 5 minutes before serving. Makes 12.

Bacon-Cheddar Balls

Linda Belon, Steubenville, OH

6 slices bacon, chopped
8-oz. pkg. Cheddar cheese,
  cubed
1/4 c. butter, cubed
2 T. fresh parsley, chopped
2 T. green onions, chopped

2 T. hot banana pepper
  rings
1/4 c. toasted pecans, finely
  chopped
assorted crackers

Cook bacon until crisp; drain, reserving one tablespoon drippings. In a blender or food processor, blend cheese, butter, parsley, green onions and pepper rings. Add bacon and reserved drippings; process until bacon is finely chopped. Chill mixture 3 hours, or until firm. Form mixture into one-inch balls. Roll balls in chopped pecans. Store in refrigerator up to 2 days before serving. Serve with crackers. Makes 2 dozen balls.

Quick tip

Out of dry bread crumbs for a recipe? Substitute dried crushed stuffing mix instead, and it will be just as tasty.

Bacon-Cheddar Balls

Quick tip

Keep favorite busy-day recipes right at
your fingertips...store them in a vintage
tin lunchbox.

Italian Egg Rolls

Pepperoni Pizza Muffins
Andrea Gordon, Lewis Center, OH

1-1/3 c. all-purpose flour
1 c. whole-wheat flour
1 t. baking soda
1/2 t. Italian seasoning
1 t. pizza seasoning

1-3/4 c. spaghetti sauce
1/4 c. milk
3 T. olive oil
1 egg, beaten
1-1/2 c. pepperoni, chopped

8-oz. pkg. shredded mozzarella
  cheese
1/2 to 1 c. grated Parmesan cheese

Mix together all ingredients. Fill lightly greased muffin cups 2/3 full. Bake at 400 degrees for 20 minutes, or until golden. Makes one dozen.

Italian Egg Rolls
Carolyn Scilanbro, Hampton, VA

1/2 c. onion, chopped
1/2 c. green pepper, chopped
2 t. oil
1 lb. ground sweet or hot Italian
  pork sausage

2 10-oz. pkgs. frozen spinach,
  thawed and drained
1/2 c. grated Parmesan cheese
3 c. shredded mozzarella cheese

1/2 t. garlic powder
14-oz. pkg. egg roll wrappers
olive oil for deep frying
Garnish: pizza sauce, warmed

In a skillet over medium heat, sauté onion and green pepper in oil. Remove to a medium bowl and set aside. Brown sausage in skillet; drain and combine with onion mixture. Add spinach, cheeses and garlic powder; mix well. Top each egg roll wrapper with 3 tablespoons of mixture; roll up, following directions on egg roll package. Heat 3 to 4 inches oil in a deep fryer. Add egg rolls, a few at a time, frying until golden. Drain on paper towels. Serve warm with pizza sauce for dipping. Makes 8.

Roast Beef Wraps
Nancy Wise, Little Rock, AR

1 c. sour cream
2 T. prepared horseradish
1 T. Dijon mustard
5 8-inch flour tortillas

30 fresh spinach leaves, stems removed
10 roast beef slices
1 c. shredded Cheddar cheese

Combine sour cream, horseradish and Dijon mustard; blend until creamy. Spread mixture equally on each tortilla and layer on several spinach leaves. Place 2 slices of roast beef over spinach; sprinkle on cheese. Fold opposite edges of the tortilla toward the center over the filling then begin rolling one of the open ends toward the opposite edge, rolling tightly. Refrigerate for 2 hours. Before serving, slice each tortilla into 2-inch pieces or in half for larger appetizers. Makes 3 dozen.

Mini Sausage Tarts
Wanda Boykin, Lewisburg, TN

1 lb. ground pork sausage, browned and drained
8-oz. pkg. shredded Mexican-blend cheese
3/4 c. ranch salad dressing

2 T. chopped black olives
4 pkgs. 15-count frozen mini phyllo cups
Optional: diced red pepper, diced black olives

Combine sausage, cheese, salad dressing and olives; blend well. Divide among phyllo cups; arrange on ungreased baking sheets. If desired, sprinkle with diced pepper and black olives. Bake at 350 degrees for 10 to 12 minutes. Makes 5 dozen.

Hot Antipasto Squares
Deborah Byrne, Clinton, CT

2 8-oz. tubes crescent rolls, divided
1/4 lb. cooked ham, thinly sliced
1/4 lb. Swiss cheese, thinly sliced
1/4 lb. salami, thinly sliced
1/4 lb. provolone cheese, thinly sliced

1/4 lb. pepperoni, thinly sliced
2 eggs, beaten
7-oz. jar roasted red peppers, drained and chopped
grated Parmesan cheese

Unroll one package of crescent rolls; press into an ungreased 13"x9" baking pan, sealing edges. Layer the meats and cheeses in the order given; lightly press down. Combine eggs, peppers and Parmesan cheese in a small mixing bowl; pour over pepperoni layer. Unroll remaining crescent rolls; shape into a 13"x9" rectangle, pressing seams together gently. Carefully lay it on top of the egg mixture; cover with aluminum foil. Bake at 350 degrees for 30 minutes; uncover, reduce heat to 250 degrees and bake an additional 30 minutes. Cool; cut into squares to serve. Makes 2 dozen.

Mini Sausage Tarts

Crunchy Cashew Mix

Quick tip

Clever party favors in a jiffy! Spoon party mix into empty cardboard tubes. Wrap each tube in colorful tissue paper and secure the open ends with curling ribbon... all ready for guests to take home.

Cranberry-Orange Snack Mix

Mary Ann Nemecek, Springfield, IL

2 c. bite-size crispy oat cereal
  squares
2 c. mini pretzels
1 c. whole almonds
1/4 c. butter, melted

1/3 c. frozen orange juice
  concentrate, thawed
3 T. brown sugar, packed
1 t. cinnamon
3/4 t. ground ginger

1/4 t. nutmeg
2/3 c. sweetened, dried
  cranberries

Combine cereal, pretzels and almonds in a large bowl; set aside. Stir together melted butter, orange juice, brown sugar and spices until blended. Pour over cereal mixture; stir well to coat. Spread in a 13"x9" baking pan sprayed with non-stick vegetable spray. Bake at 250 degrees for 50 minutes, stirring every 10 minutes. Remove from oven and stir in cranberries. Place baking pan on a wire rack; let cool until mixture is crisp. Store in airtight containers. Makes about 8 cups.

Crunchy Cashew Mix

Denise Faust, LaFontaine, IN

9 c. crispy corn or rice cereal
  squares
9-oz. can cashews
2 c. sweetened flaked coconut

1/2 c. butter
1/2 c. corn syrup
1 c. brown sugar, packed

1 t. vanilla extract
1/2 t. baking soda

Combine cereal, cashews and coconut in a large heat-proof bowl; set aside. Melt butter in a large saucepan over medium heat; add corn syrup and brown sugar. Stir well and bring to a boil; boil for 5 minutes. Remove from heat; stir in vanilla and baking soda. Pour over cereal mixture; stir well to coat. Pour mixture out onto a greased 15"x10" jelly-roll pan. Bake at 250 degrees for one hour, stirring every 15 minutes. Store in an airtight container. Makes about 25 servings.

Honey-Rum Pretzels

Rebekah Tank, Mount Calvary, WI

1/2 c. brown sugar, packed
1/4 c. butter, sliced
1 T. honey

1/4 t. salt
1/4 t. baking soda
1/8 t. rum extract

1/8 t. maple extract
6 c. mini twist pretzels

In a large microwave-safe bowl, combine brown sugar, butter and honey. Microwave on high for 45 seconds to one minute, until butter melts. Stir; microwave about 30 seconds longer, until mixture boils. Immediately stir in salt, baking soda and extracts. Stir in pretzels. Microwave for 20 to 30 seconds. Stir until well coated. Spread on wax paper. Cool before serving. Makes 6 to 8 cups.

Garlic Pretzels

Jo Anne Hayon, Sheboygan, WI

4 12-oz. pkgs. Bavarian-style
   pretzels, coarsely broken

12-oz. bottle butter-flavored
   popping oil

2 1-1/2 oz. pkgs. onion soup mix
2 t. garlic powder

Place pretzels in a large roasting pan; set aside. Combine remaining ingredients; pour over pretzels to coat. Bake at 350 degrees for 20 minutes, stirring every 5 minutes. Lay on paper towels to cool. Makes 6 cups.

Cayenne Pretzels

Dan Campbell, Dayton, OH

1 c. oil
1-oz. pkg. ranch dressing mix
1 t. garlic salt

1-1/2 t. cayenne pepper
1/2 t. hot pepper sauce
1/4 t. black pepper

2 10-oz. pkgs. pretzel twists

Mix together everything except for the pretzels. Pour over pretzels in a large bowl. Stir until well coated; spread onto ungreased baking sheets. Bake at 200 degrees for 1-1/4 to 1-1/2 hours. Cool; store in an airtight container. Makes 8 to 10 cups.

Garlic Pretzels

Quick tip

Ready-set-go snacks! When you need a little something extra for guests, but time is short, just pick up a few nibblers at the store. Assorted olives, fancy nuts, cream cheese and crackers, cubed cheese and shrimp cocktail all make quick & easy treats.

Jo Ann's Holiday Brie

Jo Ann's Holiday Brie

Jo Ann

13.2-oz. pkg. Brie cheese

1/4 c. caramel ice cream topping

1/2 c. sweetened dried cranberries

1/2 c. dried apricots, chopped

1/2 c. chopped pecans

1 loaf crusty French bread, sliced, toasted and buttered

Place cheese on an ungreased microwave-safe serving plate; microwave on high setting for 10 to 15 seconds. Cut out a wedge to see if center is soft. If center is still firm, return to microwave for another 5 to 10 seconds, until cheese is soft and spreadable. Watch carefully, as center will begin to melt quickly. Drizzle with caramel topping; sprinkle with fruits and nuts. Serve with toasted slices of crusty French bread. Makes 6 to 8 servings.

Great Pumpkin Dip

Jenny Sarbacker, Madison, WI

15-oz. can pumpkin

15-oz. jar creamy peanut butter

1-1/2 c. brown sugar, packed

2 t. vanilla extract

1/8 t. cinnamon

1/8 t. nutmeg

apple slices

In a large bowl, mix all ingredients except apples until smooth. Cover and refrigerate at least 30 minutes before serving. Serve with apple slices. Serves 10.

Pumpkin Dip

Missy Backues, Jefferson City, MO

2 8-oz. pkgs. cream cheese, softened

15-oz. can pumpkin

1/2 t. pumpkin pie spice

1/4 t. nutmeg

1/2 t. cinnamon

1 lb. powdered sugar

Blend cream cheese with an electric mixer on low speed until smooth. Add pumpkin and spices to cream cheese mixture; beat until smooth. Fold in powdered sugar. Chill before serving. Makes about 6 cups.

Party Food

Creamy Dill Dip

Donna Phair, Pittsfield, MA

1 c. mayonnaise
1 c. sour cream
2 T. dill weed

2 T. Beau Monde
  seasoning
1 T. onion, minced

Combine ingredients; mix well. Cover and refrigerate for 2 to 3 hours before serving. Makes about 2 cups.

Hot Feta Artichoke Dip

Teresa Mulhern, University Heights, OH

14-oz. can artichokes,
  drained and chopped
2-oz. jar pimentos, drained
  and chopped
8-oz. pkg. crumbled feta
  cheese

1 clove garlic, minced
1/2 c. grated Parmesan
  cheese
1 c. mayonnaise
assorted snack crackers or
  tortilla chips

Mix all ingredients except crackers or chips. Spread in an ungreased 9" pie plate. Bake at 350 degrees for 20 to 25 minutes, until golden and bubbly. Serve with crackers or chips. Makes about 3 cups.

Marinated Garlic Olives

Sharon Velenosi, Stanton, CA

2 c. green olives, drained
1 to 2 cloves garlic,
  slivered
3 thin slices lemon
1 t. whole peppercorns

3 bay leaves
1/4 c. wine vinegar
1/4 to 1/2 c. olive oil

In a wide-mouthed jar with a lid, combine all ingredients except oil. Add enough oil to cover ingredients. Secure lid. Refrigerate at least 24 hours to blend flavors before serving. Makes 2 cups.

Quick tip

Dip to go! Spoon some creamy vegetable dip into a tall plastic cup and add crunchy celery and carrot sticks. Add a lid and the snack is ready to tote. Be sure to keep it chilled.

Marinated Garlic Olives

Bacon-Horseradish Dip

Bacon-Horseradish Dip

Kathy Grashoff, Fort Wayne, IN

3 8-oz. pkgs. cream
  cheese, softened
12-oz. pkg. shredded
  Cheddar cheese
1 c. half-and-half
1/3 c. green onion,
  chopped
3 cloves garlic, minced

3 T. prepared
  horseradish
1 T. Worcestershire sauce
1/2 t. pepper
12 slices bacon, crisply
  cooked and crumbled
bagel chips or assorted
  crackers

Combine all ingredients except bacon and chips or
crackers in a slow cooker. Cover and cook on low
setting for 4 to 5 hours, or on high setting for 2 to
2-1/2 hours, stirring once halfway through. Just before
serving, stir in bacon. Serve with bagel chips or crackers.
Makes 7 to 8 cups.

Calico Corn Salsa

Bonnie Weber, West Palm Beach, FL

2 15-oz. cans corn,
  drained
2 16-oz. cans black beans,
  drained and rinsed
1 green pepper, diced
1 onion, diced
1 bunch arugula, torn

6-oz. can black olives,
  drained and chopped
1 tomato, chopped
8-oz. bottle Italian
  salad dressing
salt and pepper to taste

In a large bowl, combine all ingredients; cover and
refrigerate until chilled. Toss gently before serving.
Serves 8 to 10.

Garlic & Chive Cheese Spread

Kathy Solka, Ishpeming, MI

8-oz. pkg. cream cheese,
  softened
1 c. ricotta cheese
2 cloves garlic, minced
2 T. fresh chives, minced
1 t. dried thyme

1 t. dried oregano
1 t. Worcestershire sauce
cut-up vegetables, bread
  sticks or assorted
  crackers

Combine all ingredients except cut-up vegetables, bread
sticks or assorted crackers, blending well. Serve with
cut-up vegetables, bread sticks or assorted crackers.
Makes 2 cups.

Quick tip

When freezing leftover diced peppers,
corn or fresh herbs, add a little olive
oil to the plastic zipping bag and
shake. The oil will help keep the food
separate and fresher too...all ready to
drop into sauces and salsas!

Touchdown Pinwheels

Touchdown Pinwheels

Roberta Steele, Rock Hall, MD

2 8-oz. pkgs. cream cheese,
   softened
1-oz. pkg. ranch salad
   dressing mix
2 green onions, chopped

5 12-inch flour tortillas
3/4 c. green olives with
   pimentos, chopped
3/4 c. black olives, chopped

4-1/2 oz. can chopped green
   chiles, drained
4-oz. jar chopped pimentos,
   drained

Combine cream cheese, dressing mix and onions. Blend well; spread evenly over one side of each tortilla. Stir together olives, chiles and pimentos; spoon over cream cheese mixture. Roll up each tortilla jelly-roll style; wrap each in plastic wrap. Chill for at least 2 hours; cut into one-inch slices. Makes about 4 dozen.

High Rollers

Michelle Sheridan, Upper Arlington, OH

6 12-inch flour tortillas
2 8-oz. containers honey-nut cream cheese spread

3 c. baby spinach leaves
9-oz. pkg. deli oven-roasted turkey slices

6-oz. pkg. sweetened dried cranberries
Optional: seedless grapes

For each roll-up, spread a tortilla with 2 tablespoons cream cheese. Layer with spinach leaves; add 2 slices turkey to cover most of spinach. Spread another tablespoon cream cheese over turkey; sprinkle with one to 2 tablespoons cranberries. Roll up tightly; secure with a toothpick. Place tortilla rolls seam-side down on a tray; cover and chill for one to 2 hours. At serving time, trim off ends of rolls; slice 1/2-inch thick. Garnish with grapes, if desired. Makes about 5 dozen.

High Rollers

Caramel Apple Dip

Caramel Apple Dip

Jennifer Hatridge, Georgetown, ME

8-oz. pkg. cream cheese, softened

1 c. brown sugar, packed

1 t. vanilla extract

Cream ingredients together; cover and refrigerate overnight. Serve cold. Makes about 2 cups.

Apple-Cheese Fondue

Weda Mosellie, Phillipsburg, NJ

1 clove garlic, minced

1 c. dry white wine or apple juice

1/2 lb. Gruyère cheese, shredded

1/2 lb. Swiss cheese, diced

2 T. cornstarch

1/8 t. nutmeg

1/8 t. pepper

1 French baguette, torn into bite-size pieces

2 apples, quartered, cored and sliced

In a fondue pot or saucepan over medium heat, combine all ingredients except bread and apples. Bring to a simmer, stirring constantly, until cheese is melted. Serve with baguette and apple slices for dipping. Makes 4 servings.

Apple-Pecan Log

Lisa Ann Panzino DiNunzio, Vineland, NJ

8-oz. pkg. cream cheese, softened

1/2 c. tart apple, peeled, cored and finely chopped

3/4 c. chopped pecans, toasted and divided

1/4 t. cinnamon

tortilla chips, snack crackers, butter cookies, apple slices, pretzels

Combine cream cheese, apple, 1/4 cup pecans and cinnamon; form into a log. Roll log in remaining pecans; cover with plastic wrap and chill for 3 to 5 hours, or overnight. Let stand at room temperature for 20 minutes before serving. Serve with a variety of dippers. Makes 6 to 8 servings.

Quick side

For the easiest-ever snack mix, toss together equal amounts of sweetened dried cranberries, salted peanuts and chocolate chips.

Deluxe Cocktail Sausages

Carrie Helke, Schofield, WI

1/2 c. butter
3 T. brown sugar, packed
3 T. honey

1/2 c. chopped pecans
8-oz. tube refrigerated crescent
   rolls, separated

24 mini smoked cocktail sausages

Preheat oven to 400 degrees. As oven is warming, melt butter in oven in a 13"x9" glass baking pan. When butter is melted, add brown sugar, honey and pecans; stir to coat bottom of the pan. Slice each crescent roll triangle into thirds. Roll each smaller triangle around one sausage. Place on butter mixture, seam-side down. Bake, uncovered, at 400 degrees for 15 minutes, or until golden. Makes 2 dozen.

Maple-Glazed Frankies

Jenny Young, Galena, OH

1 T. butter, sliced
1 T. soy sauce

1/4 c. pure maple syrup

14-oz. pkg. mini cocktail wieners

In a saucepan over medium-low heat, stir together butter, soy sauce and maple syrup until slightly thickened. Add wieners and heat through. Makes about 3-1/2 dozen.

Deluxe Cocktail Sausages

Quick tip

Stock up on festive party napkins, candles and table decorations at post-holiday sales. Tuck them away in a big box...you'll be all set to turn a casual get-together into a party.

7-Layer Mexican D

7-Layer Mexican Dip
Renee Purdy, Mount Vernon, OH

16-oz. can refried beans
2 c. sour cream
1-1/4 oz. pkg. taco seasoning mix
2 avocados, pitted, peeled and mashed
2 t. lemon juice

3 cloves garlic, minced
2 c. shredded Cheddar cheese
4 green onions, diced
1/4 c. black olives, sliced
1 tomato, diced
tortilla chips

Spread beans in the bottom of a 10" round or square clear glass dish; set aside. Combine sour cream and seasoning mix; spread over beans. Mix avocados, lemon juice and garlic; layer over sour cream mixture. Sprinkle with cheese; top with onions, olives and tomato. Serve with tortilla chips. Serves 8.

Taco Joe Dip
Renae Scheiderer, Beallsville, OH

16-oz. can kidney beans, drained and rinsed
15-1/4 oz. can corn, drained
15-oz. can black beans, drained and rinsed
14-1/2 oz. can stewed tomatoes

8-oz. can tomato sauce
4-oz. can diced green chiles, drained
1-1/4 oz. pkg. taco seasoning mix
1/2 c. onion, chopped
tortilla chips

In a slow cooker, combine all ingredients except tortilla chips. Cover and cook on low setting for 5 to 7 hours. Serve with tortilla chips. Makes about 7 cups.

Texas Salsa
Vickie

2 14-1/2 oz. cans stewed tomatoes
1/4 c. canned diced green chiles, or to taste
1/2 onion, chopped

juice of 1/2 lime
1 t. garlic, minced
3 T. fresh cilantro, chopped
1 t. chili powder
1 t. salt

Place all ingredients in a blender or food processor. Pulse on low to desired consistency. Serves 14 to 16.

Always-Requested Spinach Dip

Jennifer Kann, Dayton, OH

1 c. mayonnaise
2 c. sour cream
4-oz. can water chestnuts, drained
  and chopped

1.8-oz. pkg. leek soup mix
10-oz. pkg. frozen chopped
  spinach, thawed and drained

1 round loaf pumpernickel bread

Combine mayonnaise, sour cream, water chestnuts, soup mix and spinach; mix well. Chill overnight. Slice off top of loaf; gently tear out center, reserving bread for dipping. Spoon dip into center of loaf. Serve chilled, surrounded with reserved bread pieces for dipping. Serves 8.

Hot Crab Dip

Brian Collins, Kansas City, MO

3 8-oz. pkgs. cream cheese,
  cubed and softened
1/4 to 1/2 c. milk

2 6-1/2 oz. cans crabmeat, drained
1/2 c. green onion, chopped
1 t. prepared horseradish

1-1/2 t. Worcestershire sauce
assorted snack crackers

Combine all ingredients except crackers in a lightly greased slow cooker. Cover and cook on high setting for about 30 minutes, or until cheese melts; stir occasionally. Continue to cook on high until mixture is smooth and cheese is melted. Add more milk if necessary; turn to low setting and cook for 3 to 4 hours. Serve with crackers for dipping. Makes about 4 cups.

Always -Requested Spinach Dip

Quick tip

A dip buffet will be fun at your next get-together! Have plenty of chips, crackers, sliced veggies, bread rounds and pita triangles on hand. Get creative and serve your dips in unexpected serving "dishes" such as hollowed-out vegetables and breads.

Quick tip

Use tiered cake stands to serve bite-size appetizers...so handy, and they take up less space on the buffet table than setting out several serving platters.

Mac & Cheese Nuggets

Mac & Cheese Nuggets

Liz Plotnick-Snay, Gooseberry Patch

1/4 c. grated Parmesan cheese,
  divided
1-1/2 T. butter
2 T. all-purpose flour

3/4 c. milk
1-1/4 c. shredded Cheddar cheese
1/4 lb. American cheese slices,
  chopped

1 egg yolk, beaten
1/4 t. paprika
8-oz. pkg. elbow macaroni, cooked

Lightly grease mini muffin cups. Sprinkle with 2 tablespoons Parmesan cheese, tapping out excess. Melt butter in a large saucepan over medium heat. Stir in flour; cook for 2 minutes. Whisk in milk until boiling, about 5 minutes. Add Cheddar and American cheeses; remove from heat and stir until smooth. Whisk in egg yolk and paprika; fold in macaroni until well coated. Spoon rounded tablespoons of mixture into prepared tins; sprinkle with remaining Parmesan. Bake at 425 degrees until hot and golden, about 10 minutes. Cool for 5 minutes; carefully transfer to a serving plate. Makes 4 dozen.

Feta Squares

Jane Kirsch, Weymouth, MA

8-oz. container crumbled feta
  cheese
8-oz. pkg. cream cheese, softened
2 T. olive oil

3 cloves garlic, finely chopped
1 loaf sliced party pumpernickel
  bread
1 pt. grape tomatoes, halved

2 to 3 T. fresh chives, finely
  chopped

In a bowl, mix feta cheese, cream cheese, olive oil and garlic. Spread mixture on pumpernickel slices. Place on ungreased baking sheets. Top each square with a tomato half; sprinkle with chives. Bake at 350 degrees for 15 minutes. Serves 8 to 10.

Pasta, Pasta, Pasta

Cheesy Ham & Vegetable Bake

Jackie Flood, Geneseo, NY

1-1/2 c. rotini pasta, uncooked
16-oz. pkg. frozen broccoli, carrots and cauliflower blend
1/2 c. sour cream
1/2 c. milk
1-1/2 c. shredded Cheddar cheese, divided
1-1/2 c. cooked ham, chopped
1/4 c. onion, chopped
1 clove garlic, minced
1/2 c. croutons, crushed

Cook pasta according to package directions; add frozen vegetables to cooking water just to thaw. Drain; place mixture in a 2-quart casserole dish that has been sprayed with non-stick vegetable spray. Mix sour cream, milk, one cup cheese, ham, onion and garlic; stir into pasta mixture in dish. Bake, uncovered, at 350 degrees for 30 minutes. Sprinkle with croutons and remaining cheese during last 5 minutes of baking. Serves 6.

Gnocchi Casserole

Chad Rutan, Gooseberry Patch

1 lb. ground pork sausage
16-oz. pkg. frozen gnocchi
26-oz. jar pasta sauce
1-1/2 t. Italian seasoning
2 c. shredded mozzarella cheese, divided

Brown sausage in a skillet over medium heat; drain. Meanwhile, cook gnocchi according to package directions; drain. In a greased 2-quart casserole dish, combine all ingredients except one cup cheese. Bake, uncovered, at 350 degrees for 25 minutes, or until heated through. Top with remaining cheese and bake for another 10 minutes, or until cheese is melted. Serves 4.

Aunt B's Chicken Tetrazzini

Bryna Dunlap, Muskogee, OK

8 c. chicken broth
2 yellow onions, chopped
2 green peppers, chopped
16-oz. pkg. angel hair pasta, uncooked
2 lbs. boneless, skinless chicken breasts, cooked
2 4-oz. cans sliced mushrooms, drained
2 c. butter
1-1/2 c. all-purpose flour
4 c. milk
6 c. pasteurized process cheese spread, cubed
Garnish: bread crumbs

In a large stockpot over medium heat, simmer broth, onions and peppers until boiling. Add pasta and cook as directed; do not drain. Add chicken and mushrooms; set aside. In a medium saucepan over medium-low heat, combine butter, flour, milk and cheese. Cook and stir until thickened; add to broth mixture and combine well. Pour into two lightly greased deep 13"x9" baking pans and top with bread crumbs. Bake, uncovered, at 350 degrees for 30 minutes, or until hot and bubbly. Makes about 12 servings.

Mommy's Pasta Fagioli

Danielle Jowdy, South Salem, NY

3/4 c. onion, diced
3/4 c. celery, diced
2 T. butter
8 c. chicken broth
28-oz. can tomato purée
1/2 t. dried thyme
1 t. dried rosemary
salt and pepper to taste
2 15-oz. cans cannellini beans, drained and rinsed
2 c. ditalini pasta, cooked

In a stockpot over medium heat, sauté onion and celery in butter until onion is translucent. Add broth, tomato purée and seasonings. Simmer over low heat for one hour. Add beans and pasta to soup; heat through. Ladle into bowls to serve. Serves 8.

Gnocchi Casserole

Homestyle Shells & Cheese

Homestyle Shells & Cheese
Kathy Mason, LaPorte, IN

16-oz. pkg. medium shell macaroni, uncooked
16-oz. container sour cream
16-oz. container cottage cheese
1 bunch green onions, minced
1 egg, beaten
2 c. shredded Colby Jack cheese
2 c. shredded sharp Cheddar cheese
salt and pepper to taste
1/2 c. butter, melted and divided
1 c. Italian-flavored dry bread crumbs

Cook macaroni according to package directions; drain and set aside. Meanwhile, in a bowl, mix together sour cream, cottage cheese, onions and egg. Stir in cheeses, salt and pepper; add cooked macaroni and mix well. Coat a 13"x9" baking pan with 2 tablespoons melted butter. Spread mixture evenly in pan. Toss remaining butter with bread crumbs and sprinkle over top. Bake, uncovered, at 350 degrees for 30 to 40 minutes, until cheese is bubbly and bread crumbs are golden. Makes 10 to 12 servings.

Pizza Pasta Salad
Julia List, Lincoln, NE

16-oz. pkg. tri-color rotini
2 tomatoes, seeded and diced
6-oz. can black olives, drained
1 sweet onion, sliced
1/2 lb. Cheddar cheese, cubed
1/2 lb. mozzarella cheese, cubed
3-oz. pkg. sliced pepperoni
3/4 c. oil
3/4 c. granted Parmesan cheese
1/2 c. red wine vinegar
2 t. dried oregano
1 t. garlic powder
1 t. salt
1/4 t. pepper
cayenne pepper to taste

Prepare pasta according to package directions; drain and rinse with cold water. In a large serving bowl, mix pasta, vegetables, Cheddar and mozzarella cheese and pepperoni; set aside. In a separate bowl whisk remaining ingredients together; pour over pasta mixture. Stir, cover and refrigerate until serving. Serves 16.

Spicy Salsa Twists
Heather Jacobson, Galesville, WI

1 lb. ground beef, browned and drained
8-oz. pkg. rotini pasta, cooked
10-3/4 oz. can tomato soup
1 c. salsa
1/2 c. milk
1 c. shredded Cheddar cheese, divided
Optional: sour cream, tortilla chips

Combine browned beef, rotini, soup, salsa, milk and 1/2 cup cheese in a large skillet. Cook over medium heat until heated through and cheese is melted; sprinkle with remaining cheese. Serve with sour cream and tortilla chips, if desired. Serves 5.

Quick tip

Keep green onions fresh longer by storing them bulb-ends down in a half-full glass of water in the refrigerator. Change the water every few days.

Pasta, Pasta, Pasta

Stacie's Spaghetti Pie

Stacie Avner, Delaware, OH

8-oz. pkg. spaghetti, cooked

2 t. olive oil

1 c. favorite pasta sauce

1 c. sliced mushrooms

1/2 c. green pepper, chopped

1/2 c. black olives, chopped

1/4 lb. mozzarella cheese, cubed

2 t. garlic, minced

1/2 t. Italian seasoning

1/2 t. seasoning salt

1/4 t. red pepper flakes

4 eggs

1/2 c. milk

3/4 c. sliced pepperoni

1/2 c. grated Parmesan cheese

Toss cooked spaghetti with oil in a large bowl; add sauce, vegetables, mozzarella, garlic and seasonings. Mix well; spread in a lightly greased 13"x9" baking pan. Whisk together eggs and milk; pour over spaghetti mixture. Arrange pepperoni evenly on top; sprinkle with Parmesan. Bake, uncovered, at 375 degrees for 25 to 30 minutes, until bubbly and golden. Let stand for 5 minutes; cut into squares. Makes 6 to 8 servings.

Quick tip

To keep your cookbook splatter-free and open to the page you're using, just slide it inside a large, clear plastic envelope from an office supply store.

Italian Sausage & Vegetable Soup

Kate Sanderson, Chicago, IL

1/2 lb. Italian ground pork sausage

1 onion, finely chopped

1 clove garlic, minced

3 14-oz. cans chicken broth

1/2 c. white wine or chicken broth

28-oz. can crushed tomatoes in tomato purée

2 zucchini, quartered lengthwise and sliced

2 carrots, peeled and diced

3 stalks celery, diced

1 green pepper, diced

1 t. dried basil

1/2 t. dried oregano

1/2 c. orzo pasta, uncooked

1/2 t. salt

1/2 t. pepper

Brown sausage in a Dutch oven over medium heat. Drain, leaving a small amount of drippings in pan. Add onion and garlic; cook just until tender. Add broth, wine or broth, vegetables and herbs; bring to a boil. Add uncooked pasta; reduce heat and simmer for 20 minutes, until vegetables and pasta are tender. Add salt and pepper to taste. Makes 6 to 8 servings.

Ziti with Spinach & Cheese

Karen Pilcher, Burleson, TX

2 10-oz. pkgs. frozen chopped spinach, cooked and drained

15-oz. container ricotta cheese

3 eggs, beaten

2/3 c. grated Parmesan cheese

1/4 t. pepper

16-oz. pkg. ziti pasta, cooked

28-oz. jar spaghetti sauce

2 t. dried oregano

12-oz. pkg. shredded mozzarella cheese

Combine spinach, ricotta cheese, eggs, Parmesan cheese and pepper; set aside. Combine pasta, spaghetti sauce and oregano; place half the pasta mixture in an ungreased 13"x9" baking pan. Layer with spinach mixture and mozzarella. Add remaining pasta mixture. Cover with aluminum foil and bake at 375 degrees for 25 minutes. Uncover and bake another 5 minutes, or until bubbly. Remove from the oven and let stand for about 10 minutes before serving. Serves 8.

Italian Sausage & Vegatable Soup

Chicken Noodle Gumbo

Chicken Noodle Gumbo
Lorrie Smith, Drummonds, TN

2 lbs. boneless, skinless chicken breasts, cut into 1-inch cubes
4 16-oz. cans chicken broth

15-oz. can diced tomatoes
32-oz. pkg. frozen okra, corn, celery and red pepper mixed vegetables

8-oz. pkg. bowtie pasta, uncooked
1/2 t. garlic powder
salt and pepper to taste

Place chicken, broth and tomatoes in a large soup pot. Bring to a boil over medium heat. Reduce heat; simmer 10 minutes. Add frozen vegetables, uncooked pasta and seasonings. Return to a boil. Cover and simmer one hour. Serves 8 to 10.

Chicken Cacciatore Soup
Kathy Unruh, Fresno, CA

1 c. rotini pasta, uncooked
3 14-1/2 oz. cans vegetable broth, divided
1/2 lb. boneless, skinless chicken breasts, cut into bite-size pieces

30-oz. jar extra chunky spaghetti sauce with mushrooms
14-1/2 oz. can stewed tomatoes in juice, chopped
1 zucchini, sliced

1 onion, chopped
2 cloves garlic, chopped
1/2 t. Italian seasoning
Optional: 1 T. red wine

Cook rotini according to package directions, substituting one can broth for part of the water; set aside. Combine remaining ingredients in a large saucepan. Simmer 20 to 30 minutes, until chicken is cooked through and vegetables are tender. Stir in rotini and heat through. Makes 5 servings.

Peas & Pasta Salad
Hollie Halverson, Merrimack, NH

2 c. wagon wheel pasta, uncooked
2 carrots, thinly sliced
1 c. frozen peas

1/4 c. mayonnaise
1/4 c. plain yogurt
1 t. sugar

1/2 t. salt
1/8 t. pepper

Cook pasta according to package instructions; add carrots in the last 7 minutes of cooking and drain. Stir in peas, rinse with cold water to chill. Drain again and transfer to a large serving bowl. In a medium mixing bowl, stir together the mayonnaise, yogurt, sugar, salt and pepper. Pour dressing over pasta and vegetables; toss to coat. Makes 6 servings.

Pork & Noodle Stir-Fry

Jean Fuentes, Las Vegas, NV

8-oz. pkg. thin spaghetti, uncooked

1 T. oil

1 lb. boneless pork chops, cut into bite-size pieces

garlic powder and salt to taste

soy sauce to taste

16-oz. pkg. frozen stir-fry vegetables

Cook spaghetti according to package directions; drain. Meanwhile, heat oil in a large stir-fry pan or skillet over medium-high heat. Add pork, seasonings and soy sauce. Increase heat to high. Cook until pork is almost done, stirring frequently, about 10 minutes. Add frozen vegetables and cook until tender. Add cooked spaghetti to pan. Stir-fry for just a few minutes until all ingredients are tossed together well, adding more soy sauce if desired while stirring. Makes 6 to 8 servings.

Pepper Chicken & Rotini

Charlotte Smith, Tyrone, PA

1 lb. boneless skinless chicken breasts, cubed

1 to 2 T. oil

1 green pepper, cut into strips

1 onion, sliced

1-1/2 c. water

2 c. rotini or ziti pasta, uncooked

26-oz. jar spaghetti sauce

1 c. shredded mozzarella cheese

In a large skillet over medium-high heat, cook chicken in oil for 5 minutes. Add green pepper and onion; cook another 5 minutes, stirring occasionally. Add water; bring to a boil. Add uncooked pasta. Stir until pasta is completely covered with water. Reduce heat to low. Cover and simmer for 15 minutes, or until pasta is tender. Stir in sauce; sprinkle with cheese. Cover and cook for 5 minutes, or until cheese is melted. Makes 4 to 6 servings.

Big Butterflies & Mushrooms

Isolda Crockett, Mossville, IL

1/2 c. butter

5 shallots, chopped

1-1/2 lbs. mushrooms, chopped

1/2 c. chicken broth

1/2 t. salt

1/4 t. cayenne pepper

16-oz. pkg. large bowtie pasta, cooked

1/2 c. grated Romano cheese

Melt butter in a skillet over medium heat. Add shallots and cook until soft. Add mushrooms and broth to skillet. Lower heat and simmer for 4 to 5 minutes, stirring often. Add seasonings; stir well and cook for 5 more minutes. Place cooked pasta in a warmed large serving bowl; add cheese and toss. Pour mushroom sauce over pasta and gently toss to coat well. Makes 6 servings.

Quick side

Roasted fresh asparagus is simply delicious...simple to fix, too. Arrange spears on a baking sheet and sprinkle with olive oil and garlic salt. Bake at 425 degrees for 10 to 15 minutes. Serve warm or at room temperature.

Big Butterflies & Mushrooms

Rainbow Pasta Salad

Quick tip

Don't worry about preparing too much pasta! Any leftovers can be refrigerated and used later in other dishes, like salads, casseroles or soups.

Creamy Ranch Macaroni Salad
Dawn Wetherington, Kankakee, IL

16-oz. pkg. medium shell pasta,
  uncooked
3/4 c. onion, chopped
1/2 c. celery, chopped

1 c. fresh Italian parsley, chopped
1 c. sour cream
1-oz. pkg. ranch salad dressing
  mix, divided

1 c. mayonnaise
1/2 c. shredded Cheddar cheese

Cook shells according to package directions; drain and rinse with cold water. Set aside. Combine onion, celery and parsley in a large bowl; add shells and toss together. Add sour cream and half the salad dressing mix; stir well. Add mayonnaise and remaining dressing mix; stir again. Toss with Cheddar cheese. Serves 8 to 10.

Rainbow Pasta Salad
Melissa Phillips, Provo, UT

16-oz. pkg. rainbow rotini,
  uncooked
6-oz. can black olives, drained
  and sliced

1 green pepper, chopped
1 red pepper, chopped
1 cucumber, chopped

1 c. pepperoni, sliced and
  quartered
16-oz. bottle Italian salad dressing,
  divided

Cook rotini according to package directions; drain and rinse with cold water. Mix together rotini and all ingredients except dressing in a large bowl. Pour half the salad dressing over the top; toss to coat. Chill. Stir in remaining dressing at serving time. Serves 8 to 10.

Chicken Parmigiana Casserole

Nancy Girard, Chesapeake, VA

1 c. Italian-flavored dry
  bread crumbs
1/3 c. grated Parmesan
  cheese
1 lb. boneless, skinless
  chicken breasts, cut into
  bite-size pieces
1 T. butter

1 T. olive oil
16-oz. pkg. penne pasta,
  cooked
26-oz. jar marinara sauce,
  divided
1 c. shredded mozzarella
  cheese, divided

Combine bread crumbs and Parmesan cheese in a large
plastic zipping bag. Place chicken in bag and shake to
coat. In a medium saucepan, heat butter and oil together
over medium heat. Add chicken to saucepan and brown
on all sides. In an ungreased 13"x9" baking pan, layer
pasta, half of sauce, half of cheese and chicken. Top
with remaining sauce and cheese. Bake, covered at
350 degrees for 30 minutes, or until heated through
and cheese is melted and bubbly. Makes 6 servings.

Bowties & Blush Pasta

Brooke Sottosanti, Columbia Station, OH

1 T. butter
1 onion, chopped
1 banana pepper, chopped
2 cloves garlic, chopped
1 T. all-purpose flour
3/4 c. milk
1/2 c. whipping cream

1/2 t. salt
1-1/4 c. spaghetti sauce
16-oz. pkg. bowtie pasta,
  cooked
1/4 c. grated Parmesan
  cheese
1/4 c. fresh basil, chopped

Melt butter over medium heat in a 12" skillet; add onion,
pepper and garlic. Sauté until tender; stir in flour.
Gradually add milk, cream and salt; bring to a boil. Mix
in spaghetti sauce; heat for 10 minutes. Remove from
heat; pour into a serving bowl. Add pasta; mix gently.
Sprinkle with Parmesan cheese and basil; serve warm.
Serves 8.

Easy Italian Chicken with Pasta

Erin Tingle, Ephrata, PA

4 boneless, skinless
  chicken breasts
1/4 c. grated Parmesan
  cheese, divided
2 T. Italian seasoning,
  divided

2 T. garlic powder, divided
6-oz. pkg. angel hair pasta,
  cooked
26-oz. jar spaghetti sauce,
  heated

Place chicken breasts in a broiler pan; sprinkle with half
of the cheese, half of the Italian seasoning and half of
the garlic powder. Broil for 5 to 10 minutes; turn chicken
breasts and sprinkle with remaining cheese, Italian
seasoning and garlic powder. Broil for an additional
5 to 10 minutes or until juices run clear when pierced
with a fork. Serve chicken over top of pasta and pour
sauce over all. Makes 4 servings.

Easy Italian Chicken with Pasta

Spinach Pasta Toss

Quick side

Try this refreshing salad! Peel and thinly slice three cucumbers and one small red onion. Toss with 2 tablespoons chopped fresh dill and one tablespoon each lemon juice, vegetable oil and sugar. Season with 3/4 teaspoon salt and refrigerate, covered, for 2 hours.

Spinach Pasta Toss

Jan Sherwood, Carpentersville, IL

14-1/2 oz. can Italian-style diced
  tomatoes
2 c. multi-grain penne pasta,
  uncooked

1 c. water
9-oz. package fresh baby spinach,
  divided

1 c. shredded Italian 3-cheese
  blend

In a large saucepan, combine tomatoes with juice, uncooked pasta and water. Bring to a boil over medium-high heat. Reduce heat to medium-low. Cover and simmer about 10 minutes, just until pasta is tender. Stir in half of spinach. Cover and cook for 2 minutes, or until wilted. Repeat with remaining spinach. Serve topped with cheese. Makes 6 servings.

Caprese Pasta Salad

Laura Fullen, Fort Wayne, IN

1 c. fresh basil
1/4 c. grated Romano cheese
1/4 c. pine nuts
2 cloves garlic

1/4 c. olive oil
16-oz. pkg. fusilli pasta, cooked
1 pt. cherry tomatoes, halved
2 T. grated Parmesan cheese

4-oz. ball fresh mozzarella cheese,
  cut into strips
salt and pepper to taste

Place basil, Romano cheese, pine nuts and garlic in a food processor. Pulse until mixture is a coarse paste. With food processor turned on, add oil in a slow, steady stream, processing until smooth. In a large bowl, combine cooked pasta, tomatoes, Parmesan cheese, mozzarella cheese and pesto. Season with salt and pepper; mix well. Refrigerate, covered, for 45 minutes; stir again before serving. Serves 8.

3-Cheese Stuffed Shells

Sharon Laney, Maryville, TN

12-oz. pkg. jumbo pasta shells,
  uncooked
28-oz. jar favorite spaghetti sauce, divided
8-oz. pkg. shredded mozzarella cheese
8-oz. container ricotta cheese
1/2 c. grated Parmesan cheese

1 egg, beaten
1 t. dried parsley
Optional: 10-oz. pkg. chopped spinach, thawed and
  well drained, additional shredded mozzarella
  cheese

Cook pasta shells according to package directions; drain. Meanwhile, spread half the sauce in the bottom of a lightly greased 11"x9" baking pan; set aside. In a bowl, combine cheeses, egg, parsley and spinach if using; mix well. Spoon cheese mixture into shells. Arrange stuffed shells in pan in a single layer; cover with remaining sauce. If desired, top with more cheese. Bake, uncovered at 350 degrees for about an hour, or until hot and bubbly. Makes 10 servings.

Pierogie Casserole

Cheryl Lagler, Zionsville, PA

4 onions, chopped
6 T. butter, divided
6 c. potatoes, peeled and boiled
1/2 c. chicken broth
1/2 to 1 c. milk

salt and pepper to taste
2 eggs, beaten
1/4 c. shredded Cooper or Colby cheese
1/4 to 1/2 c. shredded Cheddar cheese
16-oz. pkg. mafalda pasta, cooked

Sauté onions in 2 tablespoons butter; set aside. Mash potatoes with broth, milk, remaining butter, salt and pepper. Add eggs and cheeses; mix well. Layer pasta, potatoes and onions in a greased 13"x9" baking pan. Bake at 350 degrees for 30 minutes. Serves 12.

3-Cheese Stuffed Shells

Quick tip

An old cast-iron skillet is wonderful for cooking up homestyle dinners. If it hasn't been used in awhile, season it first. Rub it lightly with oil, bake at 300 degrees for an hour and let it cool completely in the oven. Now it's ready for many more years of good cooking!

New-Fangled Tuna Penne Casserole

New-Fangled Tuna Penne Casserole
Sarah Kropf, Richmond, VA

2-1/4 c. whole-wheat penne pasta, uncooked
1/2 lb. sliced mushrooms
2 green onions, minced
1/4 c. fresh Italian parsley, minced
1 to 2 6-oz. cans tuna, drained
8-oz. container reduced-fat sour cream
1/2 c. light mayonnaise
2 t. Dijon mustard
Optional: 2 T. dry white wine
1/2 c. shredded Cheddar cheese

Cook pasta according to package directions; drain and return to pan. Meanwhile, spray a skillet with non-stick vegetable spray. Add mushrooms, onions and parsley. Cook over medium heat until mushrooms are tender, about 5 minutes. Add tuna; cook until heated through. Stir tuna mixture into pasta; blend in sour cream, mayonnaise, mustard and wine, if using. Spread in a lightly greased 2-quart casserole dish. Top with cheese. Bake, uncovered, at 375 degrees for 30 minutes. Serves 2.

Chicken Stuffed Shells
Georgia Cooper, Helena, MT

6 oz. pkg. herb-flavored stuffing mix
2 c. chicken, cooked and diced
1 c. mayonnaise
2 10-3/4 oz. cans cream of chicken soup
30 to 36 jumbo shells, cooked
grated Parmesan cheese to taste

Prepare stuffing mix according to package directions; stir in chicken and mayonnaise. In a separate bowl, mix soup with one soup can water; pour half on the bottom of a lightly greased 13"x9" baking pan. Stuff shells with stuffing mixture; place shells open-side up in pan. Pour remaining soup mixture over top. Sprinkle with cheese. Cover and bake at 350 degrees for 45 to 60 minutes. Serves 8 to 10.

Joe's Favorite Pasta
Rebecca Aikens, Clarion, PA

1 bulb garlic
1/4 c. plus 2 t. olive oil, divided
14-1/2 oz. can diced tomatoes
2 to 3 t. dried basil
1/4 to 1/2 t. red pepper flakes
salt to taste
16-oz. pkg. linguine pasta, uncooked

Slice 1/4 inch off top of garlic bulb; drizzle with 2 teaspoons olive oil. Wrap in aluminum foil; bake at 350 degrees for 25 minutes. Remove garlic from oven; let stand. In a large bowl, combine tomatoes and seasonings; mix well. Remove garlic from aluminum foil and squeeze out cloves; chop finely and add to tomato mixture. Refrigerate for at least 2 hours. When ready to serve, cook pasta according to package directions; drain. Combine hot pasta with cold tomato sauce; mix well. Serves 6.

Chicken Alfredo Primavera

Jenny Unternahrer, Wayland, IA

6 c. penne pasta, uncooked

3 boneless, skinless chicken breasts, diced

2 to 3 t. olive oil

2 zucchini, diced

2 yellow squash, diced

1 green or red pepper, diced

1/2 red onion, diced

8-oz. pkg. sliced mushrooms

2 16-oz. jars Alfredo sauce

2 c. shredded Italian-blend or mozzarella cheese

Cook pasta according to package directions; drain. Meanwhile, in a large skillet over medium heat, cook chicken in oil until nearly done. Add vegetables and cook almost to desired tenderness. In a large bowl, combine chicken mixture and pasta; stir in Alfredo sauce. Transfer to 2 greased 2-quart casserole dishes; top with cheese. Wrap and freeze one dish for later (thaw before baking). Bake, uncovered, at 350 degrees for 30 minutes, until bubbly and cheese is melted. Serves 4 to 6.

Chunky Tomato Pasta Bake

Jewel Sharpe, Raleigh, NC

6-oz. pkg. rigatoni, cooked and drained

1 lb. ground beef, browned

14-oz. can diced seasoned tomatoes with green pepper and onion

10-3/4 oz. can cream of mushroom soup

1-1/2 c. shredded mozzarella cheese

Combine pasta, meat, tomatoes and soup in a lightly greased 11"x7" baking dish. Cover and bake at 350 degrees for 25 minutes; uncover and top with cheese. Bake until cheese melts. Makes 4 servings.

Warm Orzo Salad

Phyl Broich-Wessling, Garner, IA

16-oz. pkg. orzo pasta, uncooked

12-oz. jar roasted red peppers, drained and large pieces cut up

3-1/2 oz. jar capers, drained

14-oz. jar artichoke hearts, drained

6-oz. can black olives, drained and halved

1 c. pine nuts

Cook orzo according to package directions. Drain; transfer orzo to a serving bowl. Mix in remaining ingredients. Toss with desired amount of Olive Oil Dressing. Serve warm. Serves 10 to 15.

Olive Oil Dressing:

1/2 to 3/4 c. olive oil

juice of 1/2 lemon

2 T. garlic, minced

1 T. fresh oregano, chopped, or to taste

2 t. fresh parsley, chopped

Make dressing ahead of time by shaking all ingredients together in a covered jar. Cover and chill before using.

Quick tip

Keep browned ground beef on hand for easy meal prep. Just crumble several pounds of beef into a baking pan and bake at 350 degrees until browned through, stirring often. Drain well and pack recipe-size portions in freezer bags.

Chunky Tomato Pasta Bake

Italian Wedding Soup

Ravioli Casserole

Linda Jancik, Lakewood, OH

28-oz. jar spaghetti sauce, divided
25-oz. pkg. frozen cheese ravioli, cooked and divided
16-oz. container cottage cheese, divided

16-oz. pkg. shredded mozzarella cheese, divided
1/4 c. grated Parmesan cheese

Spread 1/2 cup spaghetti sauce in a lightly greased 13"x9" baking pan; layer with half the ravioli. Pour 1-1/4 cups sauce over ravioli. Spread one cup cottage cheese over top; sprinkle with 2 cups mozzarella cheese. Layer with remaining ingredients, ending with mozzarella cheese. Sprinkle with Parmesan cheese. Bake, uncovered, at 350 degrees for 30 to 40 minutes. Let stand for 5 to 10 minutes before serving. Makes 8 servings.

Zucchini Provencal

Brenda Saylor, Tiffin, OH

8-oz. pkg. fettuccine pasta, uncooked and divided
3 T. olive oil
1/2 c. onion, chopped
1 clove garlic, minced
4 c. zucchini, thinly sliced
2 to 3 tomatoes, chopped
8-oz. pkg. mozzarella cheese, cubed

1/2 t. dried oregano
1 t. salt
pepper to taste
Optional: 1/4 c. sliced black olives
Garnish: grated Parmesan cheese

Divide pasta in half, reserving half for use in another recipe. Cook remaining pasta according to package directions; drain. Meanwhile, heat oil in a large skillet over medium heat. Add onion and garlic; cook, stirring often, for 5 minutes. Add zucchini and tomatoes. Cook and stir for 5 minutes, or until zucchini is crisp-tender. Stir in mozzarella cheese, cooked pasta, seasonings and olives, if using. Cook, stirring gently, until heated through and mozzarella starts to melt. Serve immediately, topped with Parmesan cheese. Makes 6 servings.

Italian Wedding Soup

Linda Campbell, Huber Heights, OH

1 lb. ground beef
1 lb. ground sausage
4 eggs, divided and beaten
1 c. soft bread crumbs
2 t. dried oregano
1 t. dried rosemary
1 clove garlic, pressed
1 to 2 T. olive oil
2 14-oz. cans chicken broth

3-2/3 c. water
5-oz. pkg. vermicelli pasta, uncooked
1 c. spinach, torn
1 onion, thinly sliced
6 mushrooms, thinly sliced
Garnish: grated Parmesan cheese

Combine beef, sausage, 2 beaten eggs, bread crumbs, seasonings and garlic in a bowl. Shape mixture into bite-size meatballs. Heat olive oil in a large skillet over medium heat. Gently brown meatballs until cooked; drain and set aside. In a large stockpot, combine broth and water; bring to a boil over medium-high heat. Add pasta, meatballs, spinach, onion and mushrooms. Simmer, uncovered, until tender. Stir in remaining eggs, stirring only until eggs are set. Serves 10.

Quick tip

A jar of dried, minced onion can be a real timesaver! If the recipe has a lot of liquid, such as soups and stews, it's easy to switch. Just substitute one tablespoon of dried, minced onion for every 1/3 cup fresh diced onion.

Savory Shrimp & Pasta Toss

Kathleen Neff, Claxton, GA

12-oz. pkg. penne pasta, divided
2 t. olive oil
1 onion, chopped
28-oz. can diced tomatoes
1/4 t. red pepper flakes

1/4 t. dried oregano
1 lb. uncooked medium shrimp, peeled and cleaned
1/4 c. fresh parsley, chopped
4-oz. pkg. crumbled feta cheese, divided

Measure out half the package of pasta, reserving the rest for another recipe. Cook as package directs; drain. Meanwhile, in a large heavy skillet, heat oil over medium heat. Add onion; cook until tender and lightly golden. Stir in tomatoes and their juice, red pepper flakes and oregano; cook until boiling over high heat. Reduce heat to medium; cook sauce until slightly thickened, stirring occasionally. Stir in shrimp; cook for 2 to 4 minutes, until pink. Remove skillet from heat; stir in parsley and 1/2 cup feta cheese. Add cooked pasta to skillet mixture and toss to coat. Use remaining cheese to top each serving. Serves 4.

Summer Linguine

Lisa Sharman, Valencia, CA

2 14-1/2 oz. cans diced tomatoes, drained
1 bunch green onions, chopped
2 cloves garlic, pressed
1 bunch fresh basil, chopped

8-oz. pkg. mozzarella cheese, cubed
16-oz. pkg. linguine pasta, uncooked
3 to 4 T. olive oil

Combine tomatoes, onions, garlic, seasonings and mozzarella in a large serving bowl; mix well and set aside. Cook pasta according to package directions; drain and return to pan. Stir oil into pasta; add pasta to mixture in bowl and toss to mix. Serves 6 to 8.

Savory Shrimp & Pasta Toss

Zucchini & Ratatouille Pasta

Zucchini & Ratatouille Pasta

Jennifer Breeden, Chesterfield, VA

2 T. olive oil

3/4 lb. boneless, skinless chicken breasts, cut into 1/2-inch pieces

1 c. green pepper, sliced

1-1/2 c. eggplant, peeled and diced

1-1/2 c. zucchini, thinly sliced

27-1/2 oz. jar pasta sauce

8-oz. pkg. penne pasta, cooked

Garnish: grated Parmesan cheese

Heat oil in a saucepan over medium-high heat; add chicken and pepper. Cook, stirring frequently, until chicken is no longer pink. Add eggplant and zucchini; cook 3 minutes, stirring frequently, until vegetables are tender. Stir in pasta sauce and heat to boiling. Reduce heat and simmer, uncovered, 10 minutes or until chicken juices run clear. Spoon sauce over pasta and sprinkle with Parmesan cheese. Serves 6.

Cheesy Chicken-Tomato Pasta

Tonya Lewis, Crothersville, IN

8-oz. pkg. rotini pasta, uncooked and divided

3/4 lb. boneless chicken breast stir-fry strips

10-3/4 oz. can cream of chicken soup

1/2 c. milk

1-1/2 c. roma tomatoes, chopped

2 T. fresh basil, chopped

1 c. shredded mozzarella cheese

Measure 2 cups uncooked pasta and cook according to package directions; drain. Reserve remaining pasta for another recipe. Meanwhile, heat a non-stick skillet over medium-high heat. Add chicken; cook for 4 to 6 minutes, stirring frequently, until no longer pink in the center. Reduce heat to medium; stir in soup, milk, tomatoes, basil and cooked pasta. Cook for about 8 minutes, stirring occasionally, until bubbly and heated through. Sprinkle with cheese. Remove from heat; cover and let stand until cheese is melted, 2 to 3 minutes. Serves 4.

Pasta with Roasted Vegetables

Vickie

1 lb. fresh mixed vegetables, chopped

salt and pepper to taste

2 t. dried rosemary

2 t. dried thyme

2 T. olive oil

1/2 lb. rigatoni, cooked

2 t. balsamic vinegar

2-1/2 T. grated Parmesan cheese

Arrange vegetables in a lightly greased 13"x9" baking dish. Season with salt, pepper, rosemary and thyme; pour oil over all and toss. Roast vegetables at 500 degrees for 10 minutes or until browned. Drain vegetables, reserving juice; set aside. In a large serving bowl, toss pasta, vegetables, reserved juice and vinegar together. Sprinkle with Parmesan cheese; toss. Makes 4 servings.

Quick side

If you like garlic-flavored oil, try this. Peel fresh garlic cloves, place in a glass jar and cover with olive or safflower oil. The delicious oil is terrific for cooking and for salads! Remember to keep the jar in the fridge and use within 10 days.

Speedy Skillet Lasagna

Tami Bowman, Marysville, OH

1 lb. ground turkey
1/4 t. garlic powder
1/4 t. Italian seasoning
2 14-oz. cans beef broth with onion

14-1/2 oz. can diced tomatoes
8-oz. pkg. rotini pasta, uncooked and divided
1/2 c. shredded mozzarella cheese
Garnish: 1/4 c. grated Parmesan cheese

In a skillet over medium heat, brown ground turkey; drain and add seasonings. Stir in broth and tomatoes with juice; heat to boiling. Add 2 cups uncooked rotini; reserve remaining rotini for another recipe. Cover skillet; cook over medium heat for 12 to 14 minutes, until rotini is tender. Stir in mozzarella cheese; top each serving with Parmesan cheese. Serves 4 to 5.

Barb's Skillet Lasagna

Robyn Binns, Crescent, IA

1 lb. ground beef
1 onion, diced
26-oz. jar pasta sauce, divided
16-oz. container cottage cheese

8-oz. pkg. lasagna noodles, uncooked and broken
 in half
8-oz. pkg. shredded mozzarella cheese
Garnish: grated Parmesan cheese

In a large, deep skillet over medium heat, brown beef and onion; drain. Pour half of pasta sauce over beef; do not stir. Drop cottage cheese by spoonfuls over sauce. Layer uncooked noodles over cottage cheese. Spread with remaining sauce; do not stir. Cover and simmer over low heat for 20 minutes. Check to see if there is a lot of liquid in the pan; if so, leave uncovered and cook 15 minutes longer, or until noodles are tender. If there isn't a lot of liquid, cover pan and cook 15 minutes longer or until noodles are tender. Sprinkle mozzarella cheese over top; cover and remove from heat. Let stand 5 minutes. Top with Parmesan cheese just before serving. Serves 6.

15-Minute Parmesan Pasta

Judy Spahn, Canton, IL

8-oz. pkg. pasta, cooked
1 clove garlic, minced

1/4 c. olive oil
3/4 c. grated Parmesan cheese

Place pasta in a large serving bowl; keep warm. Sauté garlic in olive oil until golden and tender; pour over pasta. Add cheese; toss gently to coat. Serve immediately. Makes 4 servings.

Speedy Skillet Lasagna

Quick tip

Pour herbs and spices into your hand when adding them to a dish. Sprinkling herbs right from the container over hot food causes them to absorb steam and clump.

Springtime Pasta Salad

Springtime Pasta Salad

Becky Svatora, Fremont, NE

16-oz. pkg. spiral pasta, cooked and drained
2 t. oil
1-1/2 c. vinegar
1-1/2 c. sugar
1 t. salt
1 t. pepper

1 onion, chopped
1 cucumber, peeled and chopped
1 t. garlic salt
2 t. mustard
2-oz. jar pimentos, drained
1 T. dried parsley

Coat pasta with salad oil; drain off excess. Combine remaining ingredients with pasta. Cover and let marinate in refrigerator for 2 to 3 hours before serving, stirring occasionally. Makes 8 servings.

Artichoke Pasta Salad

Roseann Papadatos, Copiaque, NY

1-lb. pkg. corkscrew pasta, uncooked
7-oz. jar sliced red peppers, drained
6-oz. jar marinated artichokes, drained
8-oz. jar black olives, drained

15 slices pepperoni
1/2 lb. Cheddar cheese, cubed
salt and pepper to taste
1 T. oil

Cook pasta according to package directions, al dente but not soft. Drain and rinse in cold water. Add the next 5 ingredients and toss gently. Add salt and pepper to taste; add oil. Let marinate 2 to 4 hours. Makes 6 to 8 servings.

Crunchy Asparagus & Pasta

Janet Pastrick, Columbus, OH

5 cloves garlic, minced
2 t. red pepper flakes
2 drops hot pepper sauce
1/4 c. oil
2 T. butter
1 lb. asparagus, chopped
salt and pepper to taste

1/2 t. celery seed
1/4 c. fresh Parmesan cheese, shredded
1/2 lb. elbow macaroni, cooked and drained

In a large skillet, sauté garlic, red pepper flakes and hot pepper sauce in oil and butter for 2 to 3 minutes. Add asparagus, salt, pepper and celery seed; sauté until asparagus is crisp-tender, about 8 to 10 minutes. Remove from heat; mix in Parmesan cheese. Pour over hot pasta; toss to coat. Makes 4 to 6 servings.

No-Fuss Tomato Sauce

Jeff Doak, Delaware, OH

28-oz. can crushed tomatoes
2 T. olive oil

2 cloves garlic, minced
salt and pepper to taste

Combine all ingredients in a heavy saucepan; simmer until thickened, about 20 minutes. Makes 3-1/2 cups.

Bacon Florentine Fettuccine

Rick Pasternack, Ipswich, MA

16-oz. pkg. fettuccine, uncooked
2 10-oz. pkgs. frozen creamed spinach
1/2 lb. bacon, crisply cooked and crumbled

1/8 t. garlic powder
1/2 c. plus 2 T. grated Parmesan cheese, divided
pepper to taste

Prepare fettuccine as directed on package; drain, reserving 3/4 cup of cooking liquid. Return fettuccine and reserved liquid to saucepan. Microwave spinach as directed on package. Add spinach, bacon and garlic powder to saucepan; mix well. Transfer to a serving dish; stir in 1/2 cup Parmesan cheese. Add pepper to taste; sprinkle with remaining cheese. Serves 4.

Chicken & Bowties

Rosalia Henry, Hyde Park, NY

16-oz. pkg. bowtie pasta, uncooked
1 bunch asparagus, trimmed and coarsely chopped
1 lb. chicken breasts, cooked and chopped

1/2 c. grated Parmesan cheese
2 T. dried parsley
1/4 c. olive oil

Prepare pasta according to directions on package; add asparagus for the last one to 2 minutes of cooking time. Drain. Place pasta, asparagus and chicken in a lightly greased 13"x9" baking pan; mix in remaining ingredients. Broil for 5 minutes, or until top is crisp. Serves 6.

Bacon Florentine Fettuccine

🥄🍴🔪 *Quick tip*

Often, casserole recipes call for precooked chicken, ham or roast beef. For a handy recipe shortcut, stop at the deli counter and order thick-sliced meat...it's ready to cube or chop as needed.

Greek Tilapia with Orzo

Quick tip

A quick & easy substitution when a recipe calls for crispy crumbled bacon...try using a jar of real bacon bits instead.

Greek Tilapia with Orzo

Claire Bertram, Lexington, KY

1-1/2 lbs. tilapia fillets, thawed if frozen
juice and zest of 1 lemon
1 T. fresh oregano, snipped

salt and pepper to taste
1 pt. cherry tomatoes, halved
8-oz. pkg. orzo pasta, cooked

Rinse fish fillets and pat dry. Place in a lightly greased 13"x9" baking pan. Sprinkle fish evenly with lemon juice and zest, oregano, salt and pepper. Arrange tomatoes around fish; cover with aluminum foil. Bake at 400 degrees for 16 to 18 minutes, until fish is opaque and tomatoes are tender. Serve over cooked orzo, drizzled with juices from baking pan. Serves 4.

Swiss Alps Casserole

Pam Enebrad, Beaufort, SC

5 potatoes, peeled and cubed
14-oz. pkg. Kielbasa sausage ring, sliced
1 onion, chopped

Optional: 1 to 2 slices bacon, chopped
1 c. penne pasta, cooked
8-oz. pkg. shredded Gruyère or Swiss cheese

In a large saucepan, cover potatoes with water and boil until tender; drain and set aside. In a skillet over medium-high heat, brown sausage, onion and bacon, if using; drain. Combine all ingredients; transfer to a 13"x9" baking pan that has been sprayed with non-stick vegetable spray. Bake, uncovered, at 350 degrees for 30 minutes, or until cheese is melted. Serves 4 to 6.

Linguine & Veggie Salad

Jenny Dreisback, York, PA

16-oz. pkg. linguine, cooked
8-oz. bottle Italian salad dressing
1 tomato, diced

1 cucumber, diced
3 T. salad seasoning

Rinse linguine in cold water; drain and place in a serving dish. Pour Italian salad dressing on top; mix well. Fold in tomato, cucumber and salad seasoning. Mix well; cover and refrigerate. Makes 8 to 10 servings.

Ziti Lasagna

Cathy Hillier, Salt Lake City, UT

1/2 lb. ground beef
2-1/2 T. onion, chopped
2-1/2 T. green pepper, chopped
2/3 c. tomato sauce
1/4 t. Italian seasoning
1/8 t. garlic powder

1/8 t. pepper
1-1/3 c. ziti pasta, cooked and divided
1/2 c. ricotta cheese, divided
2/3 c. shredded mozzarella cheese, divided

Cook ground beef, onion and green pepper in a skillet over medium heat until beef is browned; drain. Stir in tomato sauce and seasonings. Cook and stir until heated through, about 3 minutes. Spread half of meat mixture in a lightly greased one-quart casserole dish. Top with half each of ziti, ricotta and mozzarella. Repeat layers, ending with mozzarella. Bake, uncovered, at 350 degrees for 20 to 25 minutes, until hot and bubbly. Let stand for 5 minutes before serving. Serves 2.

Ryan's Yummy Pasta Salad

Chris Taylor, Bountiful, UT

8-oz. pkg. refrigerated cheese tortellini, uncooked
2-1/2 c. rotini pasta, uncooked
1 c. frozen mixed vegetables

1 c. deli roast chicken, chopped
2 T. lemon pepper, or to taste
ranch salad dressing to taste

In separate saucepans, cook tortellini and rotini according to package directions, adding frozen vegetables to rotini pan. Drain; combine in a large serving bowl. Add chicken to pasta; sprinkle generously with lemon pepper. Add salad dressing to desired consistency and toss to mix. May be served warm or chilled. Serves 6 to 8.

Antipasto-Style Linguine

JoAnn

12-oz. pkg. linguine pasta, uncooked
16-oz. jar antipasto salad with olives, divided
3 T. olive oil
4 portabella mushroom caps, sliced

6-oz. pkg. sliced deli salami, cut into thin strips
2 c. shredded Asiago cheese, divided
2 c. fresh basil, chopped and divided
pepper to taste

Cook pasta and drain, reserving 1/2 cup cooking water; set aside. Measure one cup antipasto salad vegetables and 6 tablespoons marinade from jar; reserve remainder for another recipe. Slice vegetables and set aside. Heat oil in pasta pot over medium-high heat. Sauté mushrooms until tender, about 6 minutes. Add salami; cook and stir briefly. Add pasta, reserved cooking water, vegetables, reserved marinade and 1-1/2 cups cheese; toss until liquid thickens and coats pasta, about 3 minutes. Stir in 1-1/2 cups basil; add pepper to taste. Garnish with remaining basil and cheese. Serves 4 to 6.

Antipasto-Style Linguine

Stuffed Shells

Stuffed Shells

Brittney Golden, Aliquippa, PA

4 c. cooked turkey or chicken, diced
3 cloves garlic, minced
2 6-oz. pkgs. chicken flavored stuffing mix, prepared

12-oz. pkg. jumbo shell pasta, cooked
2 10-3/4 oz. cans cream of chicken soup
1-1/4 c. milk

In a lightly greased skillet over medium heat, sauté turkey or chicken and garlic for about 10 minutes. Add stuffing; mix well. Spoon mixture into shells. Arrange shells seam-side up in a lightly greased 11"x7" baking pan; set aside. Combine soup and milk; spoon 3/4 of soup mixture over shells. Save remaining soup mixture for another use. Bake, covered, at 350 degrees for about one hour. Serves 6 to 8.

Salmon & Shell Salad

Patricia Thomas, San Antonio, TX

8-oz. pkg. small shell pasta, uncooked
4 c. shredded lettuce
2 c. tomatoes, chopped
15-oz. can salmon, drained
1-1/2 c. mayonnaise

2 T. milk
1/4 c. green onions, chopped
1/2 t. dill weed

Prepare pasta according to package directions; drain. In a 3-quart casserole dish, layer lettuce, pasta, tomatoes and salmon; chill until serving time. In a small bowl, combine remaining ingredients; refrigerate until chilled. Pour over salmon before serving. Serves 6 to 8.

Shrimp & Mushroom Fettuccine

Dani Simmers, Kendallville, IN

12-oz. pkg. garlic & herb fettuccine pasta, uncooked
2 T. olive oil
1 lb. cooked medium shrimp
1 lb. sliced mushrooms

2 T. garlic, minced
10-oz. pkg. fresh spinach, thinly sliced
2 c. tomato sauce
2 T. chicken soup base

Cook pasta according to package directions; drain. Meanwhile, heat olive oil in a large skillet over medium heat. Sauté shrimp, mushrooms, garlic and spinach for several minutes, until mushrooms are tender and spinach is wilted. Remove mixture to a bowl with a slotted spoon, reserving drippings in skillet. Add tomato sauce and soup base to drippings. Stir well and bring to a boil. Return shrimp mixture to skillet and heat through; add cooked pasta and toss together. Makes 6 servings.

Quick tip

A simple substitution for herbs: use one teaspoon of dried herbs in place of one tablespoon of fresh chopped herbs.

Pasta, Pasta, Pasta

Tangy Scallops & Pasta

Alice Collins, Kansas City, MO

1-1/2 lbs. scallops
2 T. lemon juice
2 T. fresh parsley, chopped and divided
1 t. orange zest
1/2 t. salt

1/8 t. pepper
2 cloves garlic, minced
1 T. olive oil
9 oz. pkg. refrigerated fettuccine pasta, uncooked

In a bowl, toss together scallops, lemon juice, one tablespoon parsley, orange zest, salt, pepper and garlic; chill 5 minutes. Sauté scallop mixture in oil for 5 minutes over medium-high heat. Meanwhile, prepare pasta according to package directions. Toss scallops with pasta; garnish with remaining parsley. Serves 8.

Linguine & Clams

Elizabeth Cisneros, Eastvale, CA

16-oz. pkg. linguine pasta, uncooked
1/4 c. butter
1/4 c. olive oil
4 cloves garlic, minced
1 c. white wine or clam broth

10-oz. can whole baby clams, drained and liquid reserved
2 T. fresh parsley, minced
Garnish: cracked pepper

Cook pasta according to package directions, just until tender; drain. Meanwhile, melt butter with olive oil in a large skillet over medium heat. Add garlic; sauté until tender. Stir in wine or broth and reserved clam liquid; simmer for 10 minutes. Stir in clams and parsley; simmer for 5 more minutes. Toss pasta with sauce; garnish with a sprinkle of pepper. Serves 4.

Linguine with Garlic Sauce

Karen Brown, Palm Springs, CA

6 T. butter
16-oz. pkg. sliced mushrooms
6 cloves garlic, minced
1 t. dried rosemary
1/2 t. pepper
1/2-pt. container whipping cream

8-oz. pkg. linguine pasta, cooked
8-oz. pkg. shredded mozzarella cheese
salt to taste
Garnish: chopped fresh parsley

Melt butter in a skillet over medium heat; add mushrooms, garlic and seasonings. Sauté for 5 minutes, until mushrooms release their juices, stirring occasionally. Stir in cream; simmer until thickened slightly, about 3 minutes. Add linguine, cheese and salt to taste; stir until cheese melts. Sprinkle with parsley. Makes 4 servings.

Quick tip

A basket filled with different kinds of rolls and loaves of French bread is a simple and tasty centerpiece for a pasta dinner.

Linguine with Garlic Sauce

BLT Pasta Salad

BLT Pasta Salad

Ronda Sierra, Anaheim, CA

8-oz. pkg. elbow macaroni, uncooked
4 c. tomatoes, peeled and chopped
4 slices bacon, crisply cooked and crumbled

3 c. shredded lettuce
1/2 c. mayonnaise
1/3 c. sour cream
1 T. Dijon mustard
1 t. sugar

2 t. cider vinegar
1/2 t. salt
1/2 t. pepper

Cook macaroni according to package directions; drain and rinse in cold water. Pour into a serving bowl. Add tomatoes, bacon and lettuce; toss gently and set aside. Mix remaining ingredients together in a mixing bowl; stir well. Pour over macaroni mixture; gently toss until well coated. Serve immediately. Makes 10 servings.

Seashell Salad

Tammy Rowe, Bellevue, OH

1 tomato, diced
3 green onions, diced
1 stalk celery, diced

1 c. mayonnaise
1/4 c. French salad dressing
16-oz. pkg. shell pasta, cooked

3 slices bacon, crisply cooked and crumbled
salt and pepper to taste

Combine vegetables in a large serving bowl; set aside. Whisk mayonnaise and dressing together; pour over vegetables. Add remaining ingredients; mix well. Cover and chill. Serves 8.

Pasta, Pasta, Pasta

Chicken Sausage & Pasta

Jo Ann

1/2 c. yellow onion, minced
1 clove garlic, minced
1 T. olive oil
1 lb. sweet Italian chicken sausage links, removed from casings and chopped
28-oz. can stewed tomatoes, drained
1-1/2 c. red or yellow pepper, sliced
3/4 c. fresh basil, chopped
red pepper flakes, salt and pepper to taste
cooked rotini pasta

In a skillet over medium heat, cook onion and garlic in oil until translucent. Add sausage to skillet; cook for several minutes, just until beginning to brown. Drain; transfer skillet mixture to a slow cooker. Add remaining ingredients except pasta; stir to blend. Cover and cook on high setting for 2-1/2 to 3 hours, until peppers are tender. Serve over cooked pasta. Makes 4 servings.

Denise's Penne Rosa

Denise Webb, Galveston, IN

1 T. butter
1 T. garlic, minced
14-1/2 oz. can whole tomatoes, finely chopped, drained and 1/4 c. juice reserved
1 t. dried basil
salt and pepper to taste
2/3 c. whipping cream
8-oz. pkg. penne rigate pasta, cooked
Garnish: 2 T. grated Parmesan cheese

Melt butter in a skillet over medium heat. Add garlic and cook for one minute, until golden. Add tomatoes with reserved juice, basil, salt and pepper; heat to boiling. Reduce heat; simmer for 5 minutes, or until most of liquid is reduced. Stir in cream. Heat through on low heat for one minute, or until thickened. Toss sauce with cooked pasta; sprinkle with cheese. Serve immediately. Serves 4.

Chicken Enchilada Bake

Sara Wright, Colorado Springs, CO

2 c. rotini pasta, uncooked
1 lb. boneless, skinless chicken breasts, cooked and chopped
15-oz. can diced tomatoes, drained
1-1/2 c. shredded Mexican-blend cheese, divided
10-oz. can enchilada sauce

Cook pasta according to package directions; drain. In a large bowl, combine cooked pasta, chicken, tomatoes and one cup cheese; stir in enchilada sauce. Spoon into a greased 2-quart casserole dish. Bake, uncovered, at 350 degrees for 20 to 25 minutes, until heated through and cheese is melted. Top with remaining cheese. Return to oven an additional 2 to 3 minutes, until cheese is melted. Makes 6 servings.

Quick tip

Cut beef, chicken or pork into thin strips or slices in a snap! Just freeze the meat for 20 to 30 minutes before slicing.

Chicken Enchilada Bake

Fajita & Bowties Salad Bowl

Quick tip

Freeze leftover mashed potatoes in individual muffin cups. Once they're frozen, pop them out, store in plastic freezer bags and reheat in the microwave as needed.

Fajita & Bowties Salad Bowl

Jennifer Eveland-Kupp, Temple, PA

1/4 c. lime juice
1 T. ground cumin
1/2 t. chili powder
1/2 c. fresh cilantro, chopped
1/2 c. olive oil
15-oz. can black beans,
  drained and rinsed

11-oz. can corn, drained
1 c. salsa
2 tomatoes, chopped
8-oz. pkg. bowtie pasta, cooked
2 c. tortilla chips, crushed
1 c. shredded Cheddar cheese

Combine lime juice and spices in a food processor or blender. Process until almost smooth; drizzle in oil and process until blended. Set aside. In a large bowl, combine beans, corn, salsa, tomatoes, pasta and lime juice mixture; toss to combine. Gently mix in tortilla chips and cheese. Serves 4.

Updated Tuna Casserole

Anita Mullins, Eldridge, MO

16-oz. pkg. whole-wheat rotini pasta, uncooked
2 5-oz. cans tuna, drained
10-oz. pkg. frozen peas, thawed
2 10-3/4 oz. cans cream of onion soup

1/2 c. fresh parsley, chopped
pepper to taste
1/2 c. seasoned bread crumbs
2 T. butter, sliced

Cook pasta according to package directions; drain and return to pot. Stir in tuna, peas, soup, parsley and pepper; mix thoroughly. Pour into a greased 2-quart casserole dish; top with bread crumbs and butter. Bake, uncovered, at 350 degrees for 15 to 20 minutes, until bubbly. Serves 4 to 6.

Lazy Man's Cabbage Rolls

Ernestine Dobson, Parsons, KS

1 lb. ground beef, browned
1 onion, diced
3 T. instant rice, uncooked

16-oz. can diced tomatoes
4 c. cabbage, chopped

Simmer everything except for the cabbage in a saucepan for 5 minutes; drain. Spread cabbage in an ungreased 13"x9" baking pan; pour ground beef mixture on top. Cover and bake at 350 degrees for one hour; do not stir. Serves 6.

Vegetable Soup in a Jar

Theresa Manley, Conshohocken, PA

1-pt. wide-mouthed
  canning jar with lid
1/2 c. capellini or angel
  hair pasta, uncooked and
  broken into short pieces
1 env. instant vegetable or
  chicken broth
1/4 t. dried basil and/or
  parsley
1 carrot, peeled and thinly
  sliced
1/2 c. fresh spinach or
  Swiss chard, torn
1/4 t. garlic, minced
1 to 1-1/2 c. hot water

In the jar, layer all ingredients except water in the order listed. Add lid; use within a few hours. To serve, add desired amount of hot water to jar. Cover and let stand for 10 to 15 minutes. Serves one.

Spaghetti with No-Cook Sauce

Carla Gilbert, New Haven, CT

2 lbs. tomatoes, diced
1/4 c. onion, diced
2 t. garlic, minced
1/3 c. olive oil
1/4 t. red pepper flakes
16-oz. pkg. spaghetti,
  cooked
2 c. fresh basil, chopped

Combine tomatoes, onion, garlic, oil and red pepper flakes in a medium bowl. Cover and let stand at room temperature while preparing spaghetti. Stir basil into sauce; spoon over hot spaghetti. Serves 6.

Zippy Ziti & Broccoli

Jacob Jackson, Phoenix, AZ

8-oz. pkg. ziti pasta,
  uncooked
2 c. frozen broccoli cuts
1 clove garlic, minced
16-oz. jar Alfredo sauce
14-1/2 oz. can Italian-style
  diced tomatoes
2 c. shredded mozzarella
  cheese
2 T. Italian-flavored dry
  bread crumbs
2 t. margarine, melted

Prepare ziti according to package directions; add broccoli during last minute of cooking time. Drain; add garlic, Alfredo sauce, tomatoes and cheese, mixing well. Spoon into an ungreased 2-quart casserole dish; set aside. Toss bread crumbs with margarine; sprinkle over ziti. Bake at 350 degrees until top is golden, about 20 to 30 minutes. Makes 4 to 6 servings.

Zippy Ziti & Broccoli

Kielbasa Mac & Cheese

Quick tip

Kids love to "cook," so let them take turns selecting and helping prepare dinner at least once a week. It's a great way for them to learn basic kitchen skills.

Kielbasa Mac & Cheese
Tammy Rogers, Gordonsville, VA

7-oz. pkg. macaroni & cheese mix
1 lb. Kielbasa sausage, sliced
10-3/4 oz. can cream of chicken
  soup

1/3 c. milk
2 c. shredded Cheddar cheese,
  divided

Optional: dried parsley or
  cayenne pepper to taste

Prepare macaroni & cheese according to package directions. In a large bowl, combine sausage, prepared macaroni & cheese, soup, milk and one cup Cheddar cheese. Mix well; pour into a greased 1-1/2 quart casserole dish. Top with remaining cheese and sprinkle with parsley or cayenne pepper, if desired. Bake, uncovered, at 350 degrees for about 30 minutes, or until heated through. Serves 4 to 6.

Purlieu
Cheri Mason, Harmony, NC

14-oz. pkg. smoked sausage, sliced
  1/4-inch thick
4 slices bacon, chopped
1 onion, chopped

4 c. chicken broth
4 boneless, skinless chicken
  breasts, cut into bite-size pieces

5-oz. pkg. saffron yellow rice,
  uncooked
1-1/4 c. long-cooking rice,
  uncooked

Combine sausage, bacon and onion in a large pot over medium heat. Sauté until onion is translucent. Add broth; bring to a boil. Stir in chicken; return to a boil again. Add rice; boil for one minute. Reduce heat to low; cover and cook for 20 minutes. Remove from heat; let stand covered for 10 minutes. Serves 8.

Chicken & Dumplin' Soup
Brenda Hancock, Hartford, KY

10-3/4 oz. can cream of chicken
  soup
4 c. chicken broth

4 boneless, skinless chicken
  breasts, cooked and shredded
2 15-oz. cans mixed vegetables

2 12-oz. tubes refrigerated
  biscuits, quartered

Bring soup and broth to a slow boil in a saucepan over medium heat; whisk until smooth. Stir in chicken and vegetables; bring to a boil. Drop biscuit quarters into soup; cover and simmer for 15 minutes. Let soup sit for 10 minutes before serving. Serves 4 to 6.

Homestyle Beef Pot Pie

Doris Stegner, Delaware, OH

16-oz. pkg. frozen potato, green
  bean, onion and red pepper
  mixture
2 T. water

1/2 t. dried thyme
12-oz. jar mushroom gravy
1 lb. roast beef, cubed
pepper to taste

8-oz. tube refrigerated crescent
  rolls

Combine vegetables, water and thyme in an oven-proof skillet. Cook over medium heat until vegetables are thawed, about 3 minutes. Stir in gravy; bring to a boil. Remove from heat. Add beef; mix well. Sprinkle with pepper. Separate crescent rolls into 8 triangles. Starting at wide ends, roll up halfway; arrange over beef mixture so pointed ends are directed to the center. Bake at 375 degrees for 17 to 19 minutes, until rolls are golden. Serves 4.

Corned Beef Casserole

Sophia Graves, Okeechobee, FL

8-oz. pkg. elbow macaroni, cooked
10-3/4 oz. can cream of mushroom
  soup

12-oz. can corned beef, cubed
1/2 c. onion, diced
salt and pepper to taste

8-oz. pkg. shredded Swiss cheese

Combine all ingredients except cheese; pour into a greased 2-quart casserole dish. Sprinkle cheese over top. Bake at 350 degrees until cheese melts and starts to turn golden, about 20 minutes. Serves 4.

Homestyle Beef Pot Pie

Quick tip

Cook up perfect pasta...here's how! Use 5 quarts of water for each pound of pasta. Bring to a rolling boil over high heat. Stir in pasta; return to a rolling boil. Boil, uncovered, for the time recommended on the package, stirring occasionally to prevent sticking. Drain well before tossing with pasta sauce or a little olive oil.

Turkey & Wild Rice Casserole

Turkey & Wild Rice Casserole

Margaret Scoresby, Mosinee, WI

6-oz. pkg. long-grain & wild
  rice, cooked

2 c. cooked turkey, diced

10-3/4 oz. can cream of
  mushroom soup

6-1/2 oz. can sliced
  mushrooms, drained

1 c. celery, thinly sliced

1 c. red pepper, chopped

Combine all ingredients in a large bowl. Spread in a lightly greased 11"x7" baking pan. Bake, covered, at 350 degrees for 30 to 40 minutes. Serves 4 to 6.

Turkey Tetrazzini

Jennie Gist, Gooseberry Patch

8-oz. pkg. thin spaghetti, uncooked

2 cubes chicken bouillon

2 to 3 T. dried, minced
  onion

2 10-3/4 oz. cans cream of
  mushroom soup

8-oz. container sour cream

1/2 c. milk

salt and pepper to taste

2 c. cooked turkey, cubed

8-oz. can sliced
  mushrooms, drained

Optional: 1 c. frozen peas,
  thawed

8-oz. pkg. shredded
  Cheddar cheese

Cook spaghetti according to package directions, adding bouillon and onion to cooking water. Drain and place in a large bowl. Stir together soup, sour cream, milk, salt and pepper in a medium bowl. Fold in turkey, mushrooms and peas, if using. Lightly stir mixture into spaghetti, coating well. Pour into a lightly greased 13"x9" baking pan; top with cheese. Bake, covered, at 350 degrees for 30 to 40 minutes, until hot and bubbly. Makes 6 servings.

After-Thanksgiving Hot Dish

Amanda Walton, Marysville, OH

4 c. chicken broth

2 c. long-cooking brown
  rice, uncooked

2 T. butter

1 onion, chopped

1 green pepper, chopped

3 to 4 c. cooked turkey,
  cubed

2 c. mixed cooked
  vegetables

10-3/4 oz. can cream
  of celery soup

salt and pepper to taste

Bring broth to a boil in a stockpot over medium heat; stir in rice. Reduce heat to low; cover and simmer for 45 minutes, or as directed on package. When rice has 15 minutes left to cook, melt butter in a skillet over medium heat. Add onion and green pepper; sauté until softened. Add turkey to skillet and heat through. When rice is done, add turkey mixture, vegetables and soup to rice. Simmer for 5 minutes, or until heated through. Add salt and pepper to taste. Serves 6 to 8.

Hearty Meals-in-a-Bowl

Quick & Spicy Shrimp Linguine

Laurel Perry, Loganville, GA

2 T. butter
2 cloves garlic, minced
14-1/2 oz. can spicy stewed tomatoes
1 lb. cooked large shrimp, peeled and cleaned
1 red pepper, diced
2 green onions, chopped
8-oz. pkg. linguine pasta, cooked
Garnish: grated Parmesan cheese

Melt butter over medium heat in a large skillet. Add garlic; cook until fragrant, about one minute. Add tomatoes with juice; bring to a boil. Simmer uncovered, stirring occasionally, for about 10 minutes, or until slightly thickened. Add shrimp, red pepper and green onions; cook for about 5 minutes, until shrimp are heated through. Stir in hot pasta; toss until well coated. Garnish with Parmesan cheese. Serves 4.

Jambalaya in a Jiff

Valarie Dennard, Palatka, FL

2 T. butter
7-oz. pkg. chicken-flavored rice vermicelli mix
2-3/4 c. water
1/4 t. pepper
1/4 t. hot pepper sauce
1 T. dried, minced onion
1/4 c. celery, diced
1/4 c. green pepper, diced
1/4 c. cooked ham, diced
1 lb. cooked medium shrimp, peeled and cleaned

Melt butter in a large saucepan over medium heat. Add rice vermicelli mix; sauté just until golden. Stir in remaining ingredients; reduce heat, cover and simmer for 15 minutes. Serves 4 to 6.

Texas Hash

Sharlene Casteel, Fort Mitchell, AL

1 lb. ground beef
1 onion, diced
1/2 red or green pepper, diced
1 c. long-cooking rice, uncooked
14-1/2 oz. can diced tomatoes
3 c. water
2 t. chili powder
1 t. paprika
salt and pepper to taste

In a skillet over medium heat, brown beef with onion and red or green pepper; drain. Stir in uncooked rice and remaining ingredients. Cover and simmer over low heat for about 25 minutes, until water is absorbed and rice is tender. Makes 4 to 6 servings.

Quick tip

Add some fresh broccoli, asparagus or snow peas to a favorite pasta recipe...simply drop chopped veggies into the pasta pot halfway through the cooking time. Pasta and veggies will be tender at about the same time.

Jambalaya in a Jiff

Cheesy Baked Tortellini

Cheesy Baked Tortellini

Pat Wissler, Harrisburg, PA

10-oz. pkg. refrigerated cheese tortellini, uncooked

2 c. marinara sauce

1/3 c. mascarpone cheese or softened cream cheese

1/4 c. fresh Italian parsley, chopped

2 t. fresh thyme, chopped

5 slices smoked mozzarella cheese

1/4 c. shredded Parmesan cheese

Prepare tortellini according to package directions; drain and set aside. Meanwhile, in a bowl, combine marinara sauce, mascarpone or cream cheese, parsley and thyme. Fold in tortellini. Transfer to a greased 9"x9" baking pan. Top with mozzarella and Parmesan cheeses. Bake, covered, at 350 degrees for about 30 minutes, or until cheese is melted and sauce is bubbly. Serves 4 to 6.

Portabella-Basil Alfredo

Virginia Houser, Norristown, PA

16-oz. pkg. spinach fettuccine pasta, uncooked

1 T. olive oil

5 portabella mushrooms, chopped

3 c. milk

1-1/2 t. garlic salt

8-oz. pkg. cream cheese, cubed

3-oz. pkg. cream cheese, cubed

1-1/2 t. dried basil

1-1/2 c. grated Parmesan cheese

Cook pasta according to package directions; drain. Meanwhile, heat oil in a large skillet over medium heat. Sauté mushrooms until tender, about 5 minutes; drain any extra liquid from pan. Add milk and garlic salt to skillet; heat just to boiling. Stir in both packages of cream cheese and basil. Reduce heat to low; cook, stirring constantly, until cream cheese is melted. Stir in Parmesan cheese; cook over low heat until melted, about 3 minutes. Serve over pasta. Makes 8 to 10 servings.

Mushroom Fried Rice

Jamie Courchesne, Alberta, Canada

2 to 3 t. oil

1 c. sliced mushrooms

1 onion, chopped

1 c. cooked chicken, turkey or ham, diced

seasoned salt and pepper to taste

2 c. instant rice, uncooked

1/2 c. peas, corn or mixed vegetables

10-1/2 oz. can beef broth

1-1/4 c. water

1 t. soy sauce

1/2 t. dried parsley

In a large skillet, heat oil over medium heat. Add mushrooms, onion, meat, salt and pepper. Cook, stirring often, until mushrooms and onion are tender. Add uncooked rice and vegetables; cook and stir for 2 to 3 minutes. Add remaining ingredients. Cover and simmer over low heat for about 10 minutes, until rice is tender and liquid is absorbed. Serves 4.

Quick tip

Pour vegetable oil into a plastic squeeze bottle. This makes it easy to drizzle oil just where it's needed, with no waste and no mess.

Hearty Meals-in-a-Bowl

Easy Chicken Pot Pie

Lynne Gasior, Struthers, OH

2 8-oz. cans chicken, drained
2 13-1/4 oz. cans mixed
   vegetables, drained
2 10-3/4 oz. cans cream of chicken
   soup

1 c. milk
salt and pepper to taste
8-oz. pkg. shredded Cheddar
   or Colby cheese, divided

12-oz. tube refrigerated biscuits

In a bowl, combine all ingredients except cheese and biscuits. Transfer to a greased 13"x9" baking pan; top with 3/4 of cheese. Separate biscuits and tear each into 4 to 5 pieces; place on top of cheese. Sprinkle with remaining cheese. Bake, uncovered, at 350 degrees for 45 minutes, or until biscuits are golden. Serves 4.

Creamy Chicken & Broccoli

Carol Van Rooy, Ontario, Canada

10-3/4 oz. can cream of chicken
   soup
10-3/4 oz. can Cheddar cheese
   soup
14-oz. can chicken broth

1/4 t. Cajun seasoning
1/4 t. garlic salt
3 to 4 boneless, skinless chicken
   breasts
1 c. sour cream

6 c. broccoli flowerets, cooked
steamed rice

Combine soups, broth and seasonings in a slow cooker. Turn to low setting; whisk until smooth. Add chicken to slow cooker, pushing down into soup mixture. Cover and cook on low setting for 6 hours, or on high setting for 3 hours. When chicken is very tender, use 2 forks to shred into bite-size pieces. Return chicken to mixture in slow cooker; stir in sour cream and cooked broccoli. To serve, spoon over steamed rice. Serves 4 to 6.

Wild Chicken & Rice

Kimberly Lyons, Commerce, TX

2 6.2-oz. pkgs. instant wild rice
4 boneless, skinless chicken
   breasts, chopped
10-3/4 oz. can cream of mushroom
   soup

8-oz. pkg. frozen mixed
   vegetables, thawed

3 c. water

Gently stir all the ingredients together. Spread into an ungreased 13"x9" baking pan. Cover and bake at 350 degrees until juices run clear when chicken is pierced with a fork, about 45 minutes, stirring occasionally. Serves 4.

Easy Chicken Pot Pie

Meatball Sub Casserole

Meatball Sub Casserole

Christi Wroe, Bedford, PA

1 loaf Italian bread, cut into 1-inch thick slices

8-oz. pkg. cream cheese, softened

1/2 c. mayonnaise

1 t. Italian seasoning

1/4 t. pepper

2 c. shredded mozzarella cheese, divided

1-lb. pkg. frozen meatballs, thawed

28-oz. jar pasta sauce

1 c. water

Arrange bread slices in a single layer in an ungreased 13"x9" baking pan; set aside. In a bowl, combine cream cheese, mayonnaise and seasonings; spread over bread slices. Sprinkle with 1/2 cup mozzarella cheese; set aside. Gently mix together meatballs, spaghetti sauce and water; spoon over cheese. Sprinkle with remaining cheese. Bake, uncovered, at 350 degrees for 30 minutes. Serves 4.

E-Z Beefy Macaroni

John Bears, Reno, NV

1 lb. ground beef

28-oz. jar spaghetti sauce

8-oz. pkg. elbow macaroni, uncooked

8-oz. container sour cream

Brown ground beef in a skillet over medium heat; drain. Add sauce to skillet; spread uncooked macaroni in a single layer over sauce. Cover; cook over medium heat for 10 minutes, or until macaroni is tender, adding water as necessary to prevent sticking. Stir in sour cream and heat through. Makes 4 to 6 servings.

Upside-Down Pizza Casserole

Margaret Stears, Burr Ridge, IL

1 lb. ground beef

1 c. onion, chopped

1 c. green pepper, chopped

15-oz. can pizza sauce

1/2 c. sliced pepperoni, chopped

1/2 t. Italian seasoning

6-oz. pkg. thinly sliced mozzarella cheese

2 eggs, beaten

1 c. milk

1 T. oil

1 c. all-purpose flour

1/2 t. salt

1 c. grated Parmesan cheese, divided

In a skillet over medium heat, brown beef, onion and green pepper; drain. Stir in pizza sauce, pepperoni and seasoning; simmer over low heat for 10 minutes. Spoon beef mixture into a greased 13"x9" baking pan. Place mozzarella cheese slices over hot beef mixture. In a bowl, combine eggs, milk and oil; whisk for one minute. Stir in flour salt and 1/2 cup Parmesan cheese. Pour batter over mozzarella cheese; sprinkle with remaining Parmesan cheese. Bake, uncovered, at 400 degrees for 20 to 30 minutes, until puffed and golden. Serves 6 to 8.

Quick side

Make a fresh-tasting side dish. Combine 3 to 4 sliced zucchini, 1/2 teaspoon minced garlic and a tablespoon of chopped fresh basil. Sauté in a little olive oil until tender and serve warm.

Chicken & Peppers Stir-Fry

Stacie Feeney, Knoxville, TN

1/2 c. soy sauce
2 T. sesame oil
1 T. catsup

4 cloves garlic, minced
4 boneless, skinless chicken
   breasts, cut into 1-inch pieces

1/2 red pepper, chopped
1/2 yellow pepper, chopped
cooked rice

In a bowl, whisk together soy sauce, oil, catsup and garlic. Heat mixture in a skillet over medium-high heat. Add chicken; cook and stir for 3 minutes. Add peppers; cook and stir 5 minutes, or until chicken is cooked through. Serve over hot rice. Serves 4.

Peppers & Pierogies

Cathy Hillier, Salt Lake City, UT

10-oz. pkg. frozen potato and
   onion pierogies

16-oz. pkg. frozen stir-fry peppers
   and onions

8-oz. can tomato sauce
salt and pepper to taste

Cook pierogies according to package directions. Drain, reserving 1/2 cup of cooking liquid; cover pierogies to keep warm. Spray a large skillet with non-stick vegetable spray. Add frozen vegetables; cook until tender and golden and most of the liquid is cooked off. Stir in tomato sauce and reserved liquid; heat through. Toss vegetable mixture with pierogies; season with salt and pepper. Serves 3 to 4.

Peppers & Pierogies

Quick tip

Stock up on favorite pantry items when they're on sale...they're oh-so handy for homestyle meals in a hurry. Write the purchase date on the package with a permanent marker to make cupboard rotation easy.

Down-Home Taco Casserole

Sausage & Spanish Rice Skillet

Kathy Smith, Cincinnati, OH

1 lb. smoked pork sausage links, cut into one-inch pieces
2 to 3 t. oil
1-1/2 c. instant rice, uncooked
1-1/2 c. chicken broth
8-oz. jar mild or hot salsa
2 c. shredded Cheddar cheese

In a large skillet over medium-high heat, brown sausage in oil; drain. Meanwhile, prepare rice according to package directions, using broth instead of water. Add rice and salsa to sausage in skillet; sprinkle with cheese. Cover and cook over low heat for a few minutes, until cheese melts. Makes 4 servings.

Down-Home Taco Casserole

Kathy Goscha, Topeka, KS

1 lb. ground beef, browned and drained
10-3/4 oz. can tomato soup
1 c. salsa
1/2 c. milk
8-1/2 oz. can peas & carrots, drained
7 6-inch corn tortillas, cut into 1-inch squares
1-1/2 t. chili powder
1 c. shredded Cheddar cheese, divided

Combine all ingredients except 1/2 cup cheese; spread in a 2-quart casserole dish sprayed with non-stick vegetable spray. Cover and bake at 400 degrees for 30 minutes, or until hot. Sprinkle with remaining cheese; let stand until cheese melts. Makes 4 servings.

Speedy Sausage & Black-Eyed Peas

Narita Roady, Pryor, OK

1 lb. ground pork sausage
1/2 c. onion, chopped
1 jalapeño pepper, seeded and chopped
16-oz. can black-eyed peas, drained and rinsed

Brown sausage, onion and jalapeño in a skillet over medium heat until sausage is no longer pink; drain. Stir in peas and heat through. Serves 4.

Zesty Picante Chicken

Sonya Collett, Sioux City, IA

4 boneless, skinless chicken breasts
16-oz. jar picante sauce
15-1/2 oz. can black beans, drained and rinsed
4 slices American cheese
2-1/4 c. prepared rice

Place chicken in the bottom of a slow cooker; add picante sauce. Spread black beans over the top; cover and cook on low setting for 6 to 8 hours or until juices run clear when chicken is pierced with a fork. Top with cheese slices; cover and heat until melted. Spoon over rice to serve. Serves 4.

Chili & Biscuits

Lisa Hains, Ontario, Canada

1 lb. ground beef
1 onion, chopped
4 stalks celery, chopped
1-1/4 oz. pkg. chili seasoning mix
1/4 c. all-purpose flour

28-oz. can diced tomatoes
15-1/2 oz. can chili beans
garlic powder and salt and pepper
  to taste

Optional: 4-oz. can sliced
  mushrooms, drained

In a large skillet, brown together beef, onion and celery. Drain; stir in chili seasoning and flour. Add remaining ingredients and simmer until thickened and bubbly. Transfer to a lightly greased 13"x9" baking pan. Drop Biscuit Dough by tablespoonfuls over hot chili. Bake, uncovered, at 375 degrees for 10 to 15 minutes, until biscuits are golden. Serves 6 to 8.

Biscuit Dough:

1-1/2 c. all-purpose flour
1 c. yellow cornmeal
4 t. baking powder

1/2 t. salt
2 T. sugar
1/2 c. oil

1/2 to 3/4 c. milk

For Biscuit Dough, combine dry ingredients and oil. Stir in enough milk to form a soft dough.

Impossible Tex-Mex Chicken Pie

Carol McKeon, Lebanon, TN

2 c. cooked chicken, cubed
14-1/2 oz. can fire-roasted diced
  tomatoes, drained
11-oz. can sweet corn & diced
  peppers, drained

4-oz. can diced green chiles,
  drained
1/2 c. buttermilk biscuit baking
  mix
1 c. evaporated or regular milk

2 eggs, beaten
1/2 c. shredded Cheddar cheese
Garnish: sour cream, guacamole

In a bowl, combine chicken, tomatoes, corn and chiles. Spread evenly in a 9" pie plate that has been sprayed with non-stick vegetable spray. In a separate bowl, blend baking mix, milk and eggs. Spoon over chicken mixture; sprinkle with cheese. Bake at 400 degrees for 35 to 40 minutes, until a knife tip inserted in the center comes out clean. Garnish with sour cream and guacamole. Serves 6.

Chili & Biscuits

Quick tip

Unsure about the capacity of a favorite casserole dish...two quarts or three? Just measure out water, one quart at a time, and pour into the dish to check.

Penne & Spring Vegetables

Quick side

Serve almost-instant herbed butter with warm rolls tonight! Press a mixture of dried oregano, thyme, parsley and a dash of garli powder over a stick of chilled butter and slice.

Quick & Easy Spaghetti Toss

Sean Avner, Delaware, OH

1-1/2 T. olive oil
3 cloves garlic, minced
6 anchovy fillets, minced
28-oz. can plum tomatoes

3.8-oz. can sliced black olives,
  drained
1/4 c. capers
8-oz. pkg. spaghetti, cooked

Garnish: grated Parmesan cheese,
  chopped fresh parsley

Heat oil in a large heavy skillet over medium heat; add garlic and anchovy fillets. Sauté until anchovies are almost dissolved; add tomatoes with juices, olives and capers. Cook for 5 minutes. Toss sauce over cooked spaghetti; mix well. Sprinkle with grated Parmesan and parsley. Serves 4 to 6.

Penne & Spring Vegetables

Denise Mainville, Huber Heights, OH

16-oz. pkg. penne pasta, uncooked
1 lb. asparagus, cut into
  1/2-inch pieces

1/2 lb. sugar snap peas
3 T. olive oil
1/2 c. grated Parmesan cheese

salt and pepper to taste

Cook pasta according to package directions. Add asparagus during the last 4 minutes of cook time; add peas during the last 2 minutes of cook time. Remove pot from heat; drain pasta mixture and return to pot. Toss with olive oil, cheese, salt and pepper; serve warm. Serves 4 to 6.

Roasted Rosemary Beef

Sue Garver, Riley, KS

3 to 4-lb. pot roast
3 cubes beef bouillon, crushed

1 T. fresh rosemary, chopped
1/2 t. garlic powder

seasoning salt and pepper to taste

Place roast into a slow cooker that has been coated with non-stick vegetable spray. Add bouillon cubes and seasonings. Cover and cook on low for 8 to 10 hours. Makes 6 to 8 servings.

Creamy Spinach Ravioli

Kimberly Pierotti, Milmay, NJ

25-oz. pkg. frozen cheese ravioli, uncooked

2 9-oz. pkgs. frozen creamed spinach

grated Parmesan cheese, salt and pepper to taste

Prepare ravioli and spinach separately, according to package directions; drain. Place ravioli in a large serving bowl; top with creamed spinach, tossing to coat. Add Parmesan cheese, salt and pepper to taste. Serves 4.

Creamy Garlic & Herb Penne

Stephanie Mayer, Portsmouth, VA

5-oz. pkg. garlic & herb cheese spread, softened

1/4 c. grated Parmesan cheese

1/2 lb. tomatoes, coarsely chopped

salt and pepper to taste

12-oz. pkg. penne pasta, uncooked

1/4 c. fresh chives, chopped

1/4 c. fresh parsley, chopped

Combine cheese spread, Parmesan cheese, tomatoes, salt and pepper in a large bowl; set aside to warm to room temperature. Cook pasta according to package directions; drain, reserving 1/4 cup hot pasta water. Immediately add pasta to cheese mixture; sprinkle with herbs. Stir gently, adding one to 2 tablespoons reserved water to desired consistency. Serves 4.

Herbed Zucchini & Bowties

Larry Anderson, New Orleans, LA

2 T. butter

1/4 c. oil, divided

1 onion, chopped

1 clove garlic, chopped

1 green pepper, diced

3 zucchini, halved lengthwise and sliced

1 t. dried parsley

1 t. dried rosemary, crumbled

1 t. dried basil

16-oz. pkg. bowtie pasta, cooked

1/2 c. shredded Parmesan cheese

In a skillet over medium heat, melt butter with 2 tablespoons oil. Add onion and garlic; sauté for 5 minutes. Stir in green pepper; sauté for an additional 3 minutes. Stir in zucchini and herbs; cover and cook over low heat for 5 to 8 minutes, until zucchini is tender. Add remaining oil; toss with bowties. Sprinkle with Parmesan cheese. Serves 4.

Herbed Zucchini & Bowties

Easy Skillet Lasagna

Easy Skillet Lasagna

Terri McClure, Hilliard, OH

1-1/2 T. olive oil
1/2 green pepper, finely chopped
1 onion, finely chopped
1 clove garlic, minced
16-oz. jar spaghetti sauce
1 lb. ground beef, browned and drained
6 lasagna noodles, cooked and cut in half
12-oz. container small-curd cottage cheese
4 slices mozzarella cheese
1/2 c. grated Parmesan cheese

Heat oil in a skillet over medium heat. Sauté green pepper, onion and garlic until tender; drain. Transfer to a bowl; stir in spaghetti sauce and browned beef. In skillet, layer 1/3 of sauce mixture, half the lasagna noodles, half the cottage cheese, 2 slices of mozzarella and half the Parmesan. Repeat layers. Top with remaining sauce, making sure to cover all noodles. Cover and simmer over medium-low heat for 10 to 15 minutes. Remove from heat and let stand for 10 minutes before uncovering and serving. Serves 4.

White Chicken Chili

Andrea Pocreva, San Antonio, TX

2 onions, chopped
1 T. olive oil
6 c. chicken broth
6 15-1/2 oz. cans Great Northern beans, drained and rinsed
3 5-oz. cans chicken, drained
2 4-oz. cans diced green chiles
2 t. ground cumin
1 t. garlic powder
1-1/2 t. dried oregano
1/4 t. white pepper
12-oz. container sour cream
3 c. shredded Monterey Jack cheese

In a large stockpot over medium heat, sauté onions in oil until tender. Stir in remaining ingredients except sour cream and cheese. Simmer for 30 minutes, stirring frequently, until heated through. Shortly before serving, add sour cream and cheese. Stir until cheese is melted. Serves 16 to 20.

Red Dumplings

Elizabeth Ong, Porter, TX

1 lb. ground beef
1/2 lb. ground pork sausage
2 green peppers, sliced into rings
1 onion, sliced and separated into rings
46-oz. can cocktail vegetable juice
1 to 2 12-oz. tubes refrigerated biscuits, depending on skillet size
salt and pepper to taste

Mix beef and sausage in a bowl; form into 4 patties. Brown patties in a skillet over medium heat. Drain; add green peppers and onion to skillet on top of patties. Pour in vegetable juice to completely cover patties. Bring to a boil; cover and reduce heat to a simmer for 30 minutes. Arrange enough biscuits to cover mixture in skillet; spoon juice over biscuits. Cover and cook an additional 10 minutes, or until biscuits are done. Add salt and pepper as desired. Serves 4.

Quick side

Jazz up hot soup with savory croutons! Heat one tablespoon olive oil in a large skillet. Add a big spoonful of chopped thyme, oregano and tarragon as desired, then stir in two slices of bread, cubed. Cook until lightly golden, then garnish soup servings.

Hearty Meals-in-a-Bowl

Chicken Stir-Fry

Dylan Bradshaw, Asheville, NC

1 t. soy sauce
2 T. apple juice
1/8 t. ground ginger
1/2 t. salt
pepper to taste
1/2 lb. boneless, skinless chicken breast, thinly sliced
1/4 c. peanut oil, divided
3 c. snow peas
1/2 c. celery, thinly sliced
5-oz. can sliced bamboo shoots, drained
1/2 c. green onions, thinly sliced
1/2 c. sliced mushrooms
1 c. chicken broth
cooked rice

In a bowl, whisk together soy sauce, apple juice and seasonings. Add chicken and turn to coat; let marinate 5 minutes. Heat 2 tablespoons oil in a large skillet over high heat. Stirring constantly, cook chicken mixture in oil for 5 minutes, or until cooked through. Remove chicken mixture and keep warm. Add remaining oil to skillet; stir in vegetables and broth. Cook over high heat for 5 minutes, stirring constantly. Add chicken mixture to skillet and cook an additional 5 minutes, stirring constantly. Serve over cooked rice. Makes 6 servings.

Chicken & Sausage Supreme

Alex Hill, Columbus, OH

4 to 6 chicken breasts, cooked and cubed
1 lb. ground pork sausage, browned and drained
5-oz. pkg. yellow rice, cooked
10-3/4 oz. can cream of chicken soup

In a large bowl, combine chicken and sausage. Add cooked rice and stir well; blend in soup. Spoon into a lightly greased 13"x9" baking pan. Bake, uncovered, at 350 degrees for 20 to 30 minutes, until golden and heated through. Serves 4 to 6.

Farmhouse Chicken Bake

Vickie

8-oz. pkg. elbow macaroni, uncooked
4 green onions, sliced
2 T. butter, melted and divided
2 T. all-purpose flour
1-1/2 c. milk
1/2 c. chicken broth
4 c. cooked chicken, cubed
salt to taste
1/4 t. pepper
1/2 t. dried thyme
1 c. shredded Cheddar cheese
1 c. frozen peas, thawed
8 slices bacon, crisply cooked and crumbled
1 c. dry bread crumbs

Cook macaroni according to package directions; drain. Meanwhile, in a skillet over medium-low heat, cook onions in one tablespoon melted butter for one minute. Stir in flour until smooth. Gradually stir in milk and broth, cooking and stirring until slightly thickened. Stir in chicken, seasonings, cheese, peas and bacon. Mix in macaroni. Spoon into a greased 3-quart casserole dish. Combine bread crumbs with remaining butter; sprinkle over top. Bake, uncovered, at 350 degrees for 25 to 30 minutes, until golden. Serves 6.

Quick tip

For a healthy change, give whole-wheat pasta a try in your favorite pasta recipe...it tastes great and contains more fiber than regular pasta.

Farmhouse Chicken Bake

The Best Pot Roast Ever

The Best Pot Roast Ever

Joan Brochu, Hardwick, VT

2 c. water
5 to 6-lb. beef pot roast
1-oz. pkg. ranch salad dressing
  mix

.7-oz. pkg. Italian salad dressing
  mix
.87-oz. pkg. brown gravy mix
6 to 8 potatoes, peeled and cubed

8 to 10 carrots, peeled and thickly
  sliced

Pour water into a large oval slow cooker; add roast. Combine mixes and sprinkle over roast. Cover and cook on low setting for 6 to 7 hours; add potatoes and carrots during the last 2 hours of cooking. Serves 6 to 8.

Creamy Beef Stroganoff

Shelly Smith, Dana, IN

2 lbs. stew beef, cubed
salt and pepper to taste
2 10-3/4 oz. cans cream of
  mushroom soup

3 T. Worcestershire sauce
3-oz. pkg. cream cheese, cubed
16-oz. container sour cream
cooked rice or noodles

Place beef in a slow cooker; sprinkle with salt and pepper. Pour soup over top; add Worcestershire sauce. Cover and cook on low setting for 8 to 10 hours. Stir in cream cheese and sour cream 30 minutes before serving. Serve over rice or noodles. Serves 6 to 8.

One-Pot Dinner

Crystal Hamlett, Amory, MS

1 lb. smoked sausage, sliced
1 head cabbage, cut into chunks
28-oz. can Italian green beans, drained
2 14-1/2 oz. cans sliced new potatoes, drained
1 onion, sliced
salt and pepper to taste
1/2 c. butter
1/2 to 1 c. water

In a large pot, layer sausage, cabbage, beans, potatoes and onion. Sprinkle with salt and pepper. Slice butter over top; add water. Cover and cook over medium-high heat for 5 to 10 minutes, or until cabbage begins to wilt. Reduce heat and cook until done, about 10 minutes. Serves 4.

Quick & Easy Beef Stew

Robyn Tate, Paris, TX

1 T. oil
1 lb. boneless beef sirloin steak, cut into 1-inch cubes
10-3/4 oz. can French onion soup
10-3/4 oz. can tomato soup
1 T. Worcestershire sauce
24-oz. pkg. frozen stew vegetables

Heat oil in a large skillet over medium heat; add beef. Cook and stir until browned and juices have evaporated. Add soups, sauce and vegetables; bring to a boil. Reduce heat; cover and cook over low heat for 10 to 15 minutes, until beef and vegetables are tender. Serves 4.

Scalloped Potatoes & Ham

Lisa Quick, Clarksburg, Maryland

2 T. onion, chopped
1/4 c. butter
1/4 c. all-purpose flour
1/2 t. dry mustard
1 t. salt
1/8 t. pepper
1-1/2 c. milk
2 c. shredded Cheddar cheese, divided
6 c. potatoes, peeled, cooked and sliced
1/2 lb. cooked ham, cubed

In a skillet over medium heat, sauté onion in butter; blend in flour, mustard, salt and pepper. Gradually add milk, stirring constantly until thickened; mix in 1-1/2 cups cheese and stir until melted. Remove from heat; add potatoes and toss to coat. Spoon into a greased 13"x9" baking pan; arrange ham and remaining cheese on top. Bake, uncovered, at 350 degrees for 30 minutes, or until hot and bubbly. Serves 6.

Quick tip

After a simple dinner, a sweet & simple dessert is in order. Place scoops of rainbow sherbet in parfait glasses and slip a fortune cookie over the edge of each glass...perfect!

Scalloped Potatoes & Ham

Famous Corn Chip Pie

Quick tip

Make a double batch of your favorite comfort food and invite neighbors over for supper...what a great way to get to know them better. Keep it simple with a tossed salad, warm bakery bread and apple crisp for dessert...it's all about food and fellowship.

Famous Corn Chip Pie

Tiffany Schulte, Wyandotte, MI

4 slices bacon, cut into 1-inch
  pieces
2 lbs. ground beef chuck
1 onion, diced
3 cloves garlic, minced
2 t. salt

1/4 c. chili powder, or to taste
1 t. ground cumin
15-oz. can tomato sauce
6-oz. can tomato paste
3/4 c. water
14-oz. pkg. corn chips

8-oz. pkg. shredded sharp Cheddar
  or Monterey Jack cheese
Garnish: finely diced red onion,
  diced jalapeño peppers

In a large skillet over medium heat, cook bacon until crisp. Crumble bacon; remove to a plate and set aside, reserving drippings in skillet. Brown beef, onion and garlic in skillet; drain. Stir in seasonings. Add tomato sauce, tomato paste and water to beef mixture. Simmer, stirring occasionally, for 10 to 20 minutes, until thickened. To serve, place a handful of chips in individual bowls. Spoon beef mixture and bacon over chips; sprinkle with cheese. Garnish with onion and jalapeño. Serves 6 to 8.

Klein's Green Chili Stew

Linda Neel, Lovington, NM

1 to 1-1/2 lbs. boneless pork, cubed
2 16-oz. cans pinto beans
2 14-1/2 oz. cans Mexican-style
  diced tomatoes

2 4-oz. cans diced green chiles
15-1/2 oz. can hominy, drained
1 t. ground cumin

salt and pepper to taste

Place pork in a slow cooker. Top with remaining ingredients; stir. Cover and cook on high setting for 4 to 5 hours. Serves 4.

Hearty Meals-in-a-Bowl

Chuckwagon Casserole

Natalie Rosa, Ft. Wayne, IN

1 lb. lean ground beef
1/2 c. onion, chopped
1/2 c. green pepper, chopped
15-1/2 oz. can mild chili beans in sauce
3/4 c. barbecue sauce
1/2 t. salt
8-1/2 oz. pkg. cornbread mix
11-oz. can sweet corn & diced peppers, drained

In a frying pan over medium heat, cook beef, onion and pepper; stir until no longer pink. Drain. Stir in chili beans, barbecue sauce and salt; bring to a boil. Spoon into a lightly greased 13"x9" baking pan and set aside. Prepare cornbread mix according to package directions; stir in corn and spoon over beef mixture. Bake at 400 degrees for 30 minutes, or until golden. Makes 6 servings.

Cheesy Macaroni Skillet

Janie Richards, Phoenix, AZ

2 c. elbow macaroni, uncooked
1/2 lb. bacon, diced
14-1/2 oz. can diced tomatoes
8-oz. can tomato sauce
1 c. shredded Cheddar cheese

Cook macaroni according to package directions; drain. Fry bacon in a large skillet until crisp. Drain, leaving about one tablespoon drippings in skillet. Add tomatoes with juice, tomato sauce and cooked macaroni. Simmer over low heat until hot and bubbly, about 20 minutes. Add cheese; place lid on skillet and let stand until cheese is melted, about 5 minutes. Serves 4.

Country Pasta with Mozzarella

Bruce Butler, Tarrytown, NY

8 slices bacon, cut into 1-inch pieces
2 c. broccoli, chopped
1/2 t. garlic, minced
8-oz. pkg. rigatoni pasta, cooked
8-oz. pkg. shredded mozzarella cheese
1/4 c. grated Parmesan cheese
1/8 t. cayenne pepper
Garnish: chopped fresh parsley

Cook bacon in a large skillet over medium heat, stirring occasionally, until crisp. Add broccoli and garlic; cook until broccoli is crisp-tender. Drain; stir in cooked rigatoni, mozzarella, Parmesan and cayenne. Heat through until cheese is melted. Sprinkle with parsley. Serves 6 to 8.

Cheesy Macaroni Skillet

Fluffy Chicken & Dumplings

Quick tip

For simple table decorations, place round pebbles in the bottom of Mason jars and fill with water. Then tuck in bunches of sweet daisies or sunflowers and tie a bow around jar necks with jute.

Fluffy Chicken & Dumplings

Angela Lengacher, Montgomery, IN

1 to 2 T. oil
1 c. celery, chopped
1 c. carrots, peeled and sliced
1 T. onion, chopped

49-oz. can chicken broth
10-3/4 oz. can cream of chicken
  soup
1/8 t. pepper

2 c. cooked chicken, cubed
1-2/3 c. biscuit baking mix
2/3 c. milk

Heat oil in a Dutch oven over medium-high heat. Sauté celery, carrots and onion in oil for about 7 minutes, until crisp-tender. Add broth, soup and pepper; bring to a boil. Reduce heat to low; stir in chicken and bring to a simmer. In a separate bowl, stir together baking mix and milk. Drop batter by tablespoonfuls into simmering broth. Cover and cook over low heat for 15 minutes without lifting lid. Serves 6.

Marilyn's Slow-Cooked Chicken & Noodles

Marilyn Stonecipher, Bloomington, IN

6 chicken thighs
salt and pepper to taste
3 stalks celery with leaves
4 carrots, peeled and chopped

2 cloves garlic, chopped
16-oz. can chicken broth
2 c. water
1 bay leaf

16-oz. pkg. wide egg noodles,
  uncooked

Add chicken to a slow cooker; sprinkle with salt and pepper. Add vegetables, broth, water and bay leaf. Cover and cook on high setting for 4 hours. Remove chicken and vegetables from slow cooker; discard celery stalks and bay leaf. Add noodles to liquid in slow cooker; cover and cook on high setting for 20 minutes, or until tender. Meanwhile, chop chicken, removing skin and bones. When noodles are tender, return chicken and carrots to slow cooker; heat through. Serves 8.

One-Dish Speedy Couscous

Laurel Perry, Loganville, GA

12-oz. pkg. couscous, uncooked
2 c. cooked chicken, diced
1 zucchini, chopped
1 stalk celery, thinly sliced

1 carrot, peeled and grated
2 c. orange juice
1/4 c. fresh basil, chopped
2 green onions, finely chopped

1/2 t. salt
1/2 t. pepper

Combine couscous, chicken and vegetables in a large serving bowl; set aside. Bring orange juice to a boil in a saucepan over medium heat; stir into couscous mixture. Cover tightly with plastic wrap; let stand for 5 minutes. Stir gently until evenly mixed. Serves 4.

Luau Delight

Pat Habiger, Spearville, KS

2 T. butter
2-1/2 c. cooked ham, cubed
8-oz. can pineapple chunks,
  drained

2 green onions, chopped
1-1/3 c. pineapple juice
1 T. plus 1 t. cider vinegar
2 T. brown sugar, packed

2 t. mustard
2 T. cornstarch

Melt butter in a large skillet over medium heat. Add ham, pineapple and onions; sauté for 5 minutes and set aside. In a large bowl, combine pineapple juice, vinegar, brown sugar, mustard and cornstarch; mix well and pour over ham mixture. Cook over medium heat until heated through and thickened, about 5 minutes. Makes 4 servings.

One-Dish Speedy Couscous

Quick side

Did you buy a bunch of fresh herbs for a recipe that calls for just a couple of tablespoons? Chop the extra herbs and toss them into a lettuce salad! Fresh dill, parsley, thyme, chives and basil all add a delightful punch of flavor.

Pepperoni Tortellini

Pepperoni Tortellini

Eileen Boomgaarden, Waukesha, WI

2 t. olive oil
1 onion, sliced
1 red pepper, thinly sliced
3 to 4 cloves garlic, chopped
5-oz. pkg. sliced pepperoni, cut into strips
1-1/2 t. dried basil
1-1/2 t. dried oregano
1 t. Italian seasoning
1 t. garlic powder
1/2 t. salt
1/4 t. pepper
8-oz. pkg. refrigerated 3-cheese tortellini pasta, cooked
Garnish: shaved Parmesan cheese, fresh basil

Heat oil in a skillet over medium heat. Sauté onion, red pepper and garlic until crisp-tender. Add remaining ingredients except pasta and garnish. Cook, stirring occasionally, for 5 minutes. Stir in pasta and cook until heated through. Garnish with Parmesan cheese and basil. Serves 4 to 6.

Fresh Tomato & Basil Linguine

Jo Ann

1-1/2 lbs. tomatoes, finely chopped
3 cloves garlic, minced
1 red pepper, chopped
1 bunch fresh basil, torn
1/2 c. olive oil
1 t. salt
pepper to taste
16-oz. pkg. linguine pasta, cooked
Garnish: grated Parmesan cheese

Stir together tomatoes, garlic, red pepper and basil in a large bowl; drizzle with oil. Sprinkle with salt and pepper; mix well and toss with hot cooked linguine. Sprinkle with Parmesan cheese as desired. Serves 6 to 8.

Savory Sausage Stroganoff

Michelle Bailey, Fort Wayne, IN

1 lb. ground pork sausage, browned and drained
10-3/4 oz. can cream of mushroom soup
14-1/2 oz. can diced tomatoes
1/2 c. milk
1/4 c. all-purpose flour
4-oz. can sliced mushrooms, drained
1 t. garlic, minced
1 t. dried basil
1 c. sour cream
8-oz. pkg. wide egg noodles, cooked

Combine all ingredients except sour cream and noodles in a slow cooker. Cover and cook on high setting for 2 to 3 hours, stirring occasionally. Stir in sour cream near end of cooking time; warm through. Serve over cooked noodles. Makes 4 servings.

Hearty Meals-in-a-Bowl

Freezer Taco Rice

Patricia Wissler, Harrisburg, PA

3 lbs. ground beef, turkey
  or chicken
3 c. onion, diced
3 1-1/4 oz. pkgs. taco
  seasoning mix
6 c. cooked white or brown
  rice

3 16-oz. cans diced
  tomatoes
2 12-oz. pkgs. shredded
  Mexican-blend cheese

Brown meat in a large saucepan over medium heat; drain. Add onion, taco seasoning, rice and tomatoes with juice; simmer until thickened, about 30 minutes. Cool completely. Package in 3 freezer-safe containers; freeze. Makes 3 containers; each container serves 4 to 6.

Heat & Eat Instructions: Thaw overnight in refrigerator. Reheat in a saucepan over medium heat and use as desired.

Bayou Chicken

Dawn Dhooghe, Concord, NC

3 boneless, skinless
  chicken breasts, cubed
14-1/2 oz. can chicken
  broth
14-1/2 oz. can diced
  tomatoes
10-3/4 oz. can tomato soup
1/2 lb. smoked sausage,
  sliced

1/2 c. cooked ham, diced
1 onion, chopped
2 t. Cajun seasoning
hot pepper sauce to taste
3 c. cooked rice

Combine all ingredients except rice in a slow cooker; stir. Cover and cook on low setting for 8 hours. Serve over hot cooked rice. Serves 6 to 8.

Spicy Pork Noodle Bowls

Julie Swenson, Minneapolis, MN

8-oz. pkg. linguine pasta,
  uncooked and divided
2 T. oil, divided
1 lb. boneless pork
  shoulder, sliced into
  strips
1 onion, thinly sliced
1/2 lb. broccoli, cut into
  bite-size flowerets

2 T. Worcestershire sauce
1 T. soy sauce
2 t. cornstarch
1/2 t. curry powder
1 tomato, chopped

Cook half of pasta according to package directions; set aside. Reserve remaining pasta for another recipe. Heat one tablespoon oil in a large skillet over high heat. Add pork; cook and stir until golden, about 7 minutes. Remove pork; set aside. Heat remaining oil in skillet; add onion and broccoli. Cook and stir until tender, about 5 minutes. Mix together sauces, cornstarch and curry powder in a cup; stir into skillet. Cook and stir until slightly thickened. Return pork to pan; heat through. Divide cooked pasta into 4 shallow bowls. Top with pork mixture and tomato; toss to coat pasta. Serves 4.

Quick tip

If you're cooking in a skillet and there's no spatter guard handy, a large metal sieve can do the job. Just place it face-down over the skillet.

Spicy Pork Noodle Bowls

Taco in a Pan

Taco in a Pan

Peggy Sanders, Adair, IA

1 lb. ground beef
1/2 c. onion, chopped
1/2 c. green pepper, chopped
2 c. water
1-1/4 oz. pkg. taco seasoning mix
1-1/2 c. instant rice, uncooked

1 c. salsa, or to taste
1 c. shredded Colby Jack cheese
1 tomato, chopped
Optional: 1 c. sliced black olives
Garnish: crushed nacho-flavored tortilla chips

Brown beef, onion and green pepper in a skillet over medium heat; drain. Stir water and taco seasoning into beef mixture. Bring to a boil; stir in rice. Cover and cook for 3 to 5 minutes, until rice is tender. Sprinkle salsa and cheese over all. Remove from heat; cover and let stand until cheese melts. Top with tomato and olives, if desired. Garnish with chips. Serves 4 to 6.

Mexican Chicken

Stephanie Smith, Mansfield, TX

15-oz. can black beans, drained and rinsed
2 15-1/4 oz. cans corn, drained
1 c. picante sauce, divided

2 lbs. boneless, skinless chicken breasts
Garnish: shredded Cheddar cheese
12 8-inch flour tortillas

Mix together beans, corn and 1/2 cup picante sauce in a slow cooker. Place chicken on top; pour remaining picante sauce over chicken. Cover and cook on high setting for 2-1/2 hours, or until chicken is tender. Shred chicken and return to slow cooker. Sprinkle with cheese; cover and cook until melted. Serve with tortillas. Serves 6.

Southwestern Creamy Chicken

Jami Rodolph, Lolo, MT

5-lb. roasting chicken
1 T. garlic, minced
1 T. chili powder
1 T. ground cumin
1 T. salt
1 T. dried cilantro
2 t. paprika

1 t. red pepper flakes
2 c. water
1-1/2 c. frozen corn
1 c. whipping cream or whole milk
cooked rice

Place chicken in a large slow cooker. Mix garlic and seasonings; sprinkle over chicken. Add water to slow cooker. Cover and cook on high setting for about 4 hours, until chicken juices run clear. Remove chicken from slow cooker to a platter, reserving broth; allow to cool for about 30 minutes. Shred chicken, discarding skin and bones. Place chicken in a large skillet. Measure reserved broth, adding water if necessary to equal 4 to 5 cups; add to skillet along with frozen corn. Bring to a simmer over medium heat; cook until corn is tender. Stir in cream or milk and heat through. To serve, spoon over cooked rice. Makes 8 servings.

Quick side

Comfort foods like Southwestern Creamy Chicken are especially satisfying served over warm split biscuits or buttered toast...a terrific way to stretch a meal when there are extra guests for dinner too!

Grilled Salmon Skewers

Mary Ann Johnson, Sycamore, IL

1 lb. boneless, skinless salmon
  fillet
10 to 12 wooden skewers, soaked
  in water
1/4 c. soy sauce

1/4 c. honey
1 T. rice wine vinegar or cider
  vinegar
1 t. fresh ginger, peeled and
  minced

1 clove garlic, minced
1/8 t. pepper
Garnish: lemon wedges

Slice salmon lengthwise into 10 to 12 narrow strips. Thread each strip onto a skewer; place skewers in a shallow dish. Whisk together soy sauce, honey, vinegar and spices. Pour over skewers, turning to coat. Let stand at room temperature for 30 minutes. Drain marinade into a small saucepan; simmer over medium-low heat for several minutes. Grill skewers over medium-high heat on a lightly oiled grill, brushing often with marinade, for 4 minutes on each side. Squeeze lemon wedges over salmon; serve warm. Makes 10 to 12 skewers.

Grilled Chicken on a Stick

Donna Meyer, Lima, OH

1 c. mayonnaise-style salad
  dressing
1.05-oz. pkg. Italian salad dressing
  mix
2 T. vinegar
2 T. water

1-1/2 lb. pkg. boneless, skinless
  chicken breasts, sliced into
  1-1/2 inch pieces
1 green pepper, sliced into
  1/2-inch pieces

12 mushrooms
1 zucchini, thickly sliced
12 cherry tomatoes
6 skewers

Whisk salad dressing, Italian salad dressing mix, vinegar and water together; set aside. Arrange chicken, green pepper, mushrooms, zucchini and cherry tomatoes evenly on 6 skewers; place in a shallow dish. Pour half the dressing mixture on top, brushing to coat evenly; place remaining dressing mixture to the side. Refrigerate skewers for 30 minutes; turn to coat every 10 minutes. Grill over medium-heat for 5 to 8 minutes; brush with remaining dressing mixture. Turn and grill until juices run clear when chicken is pierced with a fork; serve immediately. Makes 6 servings.

Grilled Salmon Skewers

Grilled Portabella Blues

Grilled Portabella Blues

Marion Sundberg, Ramona, CA

1/2 c. balsamic vinegar
1/4 c. olive oil
2 cloves garlic, pressed
salt and pepper to taste

4 large portabella
   mushroom caps
1/2 c. crumbled blue
   cheese

Mix vinegar, oil, garlic, salt and pepper in a large plastic zipping bag. Add mushrooms; seal bag and refrigerate for at least one hour. Drain, discarding marinade. Grill mushrooms over medium heat until tender and golden. Just before removing mushrooms from grill, spoon blue cheese into the center of each mushroom. Let stand until cheese melts; serve immediately. Makes 4 servings.

Grilled Gouda Sandwiches

Tiffany Brinkley, Broomfield, CO

8 slices country-style bread
1 clove garlic, halved
4 t. Dijon mustard
1/2 lb. sliced Gouda cheese

2 T. butter, melted
1/8 t. cayenne pepper
1/8 t. pepper

Rub one side of each slice of bread with garlic. Place 4 bread slices garlic-side down; top each bread slice with one teaspoon mustard and 2 slices Gouda. Place remaining bread slices, garlic-side up, on sandwich bottoms. Combine butter, cayenne pepper and pepper in a small bowl; brush mixture over each side of sandwiches. Cook sandwiches in an oven-proof skillet over medium-high heat for about 2 minutes on each side, until golden. Place skillet in oven and bake at 400 degrees for about 5 minutes, until cheese is melted. Slice sandwiches diagonally. Makes 4 sandwiches.

Grilled Eggplant Parmesan

Amanda Bonagura, Floral Park, NY

1 eggplant, peeled and
   sliced into 1/2-inch
   rounds
1/4 to 1/2 c. extra-virgin
   olive oil
1 to 2 tomatoes, sliced
   1/4-inch thick, or 15-oz.
   can crushed tomatoes
6 to 7 Kalamata olives,
   chopped

5 to 10 fresh basil leaves,
   chopped
8-oz. ball fresh mozzarella
   cheese, sliced 1/4-inch
   thick
salt and pepper to taste
Garnish: additional
   olive oil

Brush both sides of eggplant slices with olive oil. Place on a vegetable grilling rack over a hot grate. Grill until tender and golden on both sides, about 15 to 20 minutes. Remove eggplant to a large grill-safe baking pan coated with non-stick vegetable spray. Arrange tomatoes over eggplant. Combine olives and basil in a small bowl; spread over tomatoes and top with cheese. Turn off burners on one side of grill; set pan on this side. Cover grill and cook until hot and cheese is bubbly, about 15 minutes. Season with salt and pepper; drizzle with additional olive oil. Serves 4.

 ## Quick tip

Gas or charcoal? Every cookout chef has his or her own opinion! A good rule of thumb is charcoal for taste, gas for haste.

Fajitas with Grilled Vegetables

Carolen Collins, Marion, OH

1 lb. beef sirloin steak
2 green, red and/or yellow
  peppers, halved
1 zucchini, cut lengthwise
1 yellow squash, cut lengthwise

4 thick slices red onion
3/4 c. salsa
2 T. olive oil
2 T. lime juice
2 T. tequila or water

2 cloves garlic, minced
8 8-inch flour tortillas, warmed
Garnish: shredded Mexican-blend
  cheese, salsa, guacamole, sour
  cream

Place steak and vegetables in a large plastic zipping bag. Whisk together salsa, oil, lime juice, tequila or water and garlic; pour into bag. Close bag securely; turn to coat steak and vegetables. Refrigerate 30 minutes to 2 hours, turning occasionally. Remove steak and vegetables from bag, reserving marinade. In a small saucepan, bring remaining marinade to a boil; remove from heat. Place steak and vegetables on a hot grill, 4 to 5 inches from heat. Grill for about 5 minutes on each side, to desired doneness. Slice steak, peppers and squash into thin strips. Separate onion into rings. Divide steak and vegetables among tortillas. Drizzle with warm marinade; add desired toppings and roll up. Makes 8 servings.

Sizzling Bacon Asparagus

Katie Majeske, Denver, PA

16 spears asparagus, trimmed
2 to 3 t. olive oil

pepper to taste
4 slices bacon

Arrange asparagus on a baking sheet. Lightly drizzle with olive oil; sprinkle with pepper. Make a bundle with 4 spears; wrap in a slice of bacon. Secure with wooden toothpicks, if needed. Repeat with remaining ingredients to make 4 bundles. Place on an oiled grate over medium-high heat. Cook for 10 to 12 minutes, turning occasionally, until asparagus is tender and bacon is crisp. Makes 4 servings.

Quick tip

Hankering for steaks on the grill, but finding T-bones and ribeyes too expensive? Try flank or skirt steak. Both are budget-priced yet tender and flavorful when marinated well and sliced thinly. Newer cuts like flat-iron steak are delicious too. Ask your butcher for some friendly tips!

Sizzling Bacon Asparagus

Grilled Zucchini Wraps

Grilled Zucchini Wraps

Teresa Willett, Ontario, Canada

4 boneless, skinless
    chicken breasts
4 to 6 zucchini, sliced
    lengthwise into 1/4-inch
    thick slices
olive oil
salt and pepper to taste

1/2 c. ranch salad dressing,
    divided
8 10-inch whole-grain
    flour tortillas
8 leaves lettuce
Garnish: shredded
    Cheddar cheese

Brush chicken and zucchini with olive oil; sprinkle with salt and pepper. Grill chicken over medium-high heat for 5 minutes. Turn chicken over; add zucchini to grill. Grill 5 minutes longer, or until chicken juices run clear and zucchini is tender. Slice chicken into strips; set aside. For each wrap, spread one tablespoon salad dressing on a tortilla. Top with a lettuce leaf, 1/2 cup chicken and 3 to 4 slices of zucchini. Sprinkle with cheese; roll up. Makes 8 servings.

Spicy Grilled Vegetables

Tina Frey, Butler, PA

3 carrots, sliced
4 potatoes, sliced
1 T. lime juice
1/3 c. olive oil
2 T. onion, chopped

1/2 t. salt
1/4 t. pepper
1/2 t. dried cumin
2 zucchini, sliced

Place carrots and potatoes in a medium saucepan and cover with water. Over high heat, boil for 10 minutes. Drain and set aside. In a bowl, combine lime juice, olive oil, onion, salt, pepper and cumin. Add potato mixture and zucchini slices, tossing to coat well. Let stand about 15 minutes, allowing flavors to blend. Grill vegetables, turning once, about 3 minutes on each side. Serve hot. Makes 6 servings.

Dad's Favorite Grilled Potatoes

Kim Henry, Library, PA

4 to 5 potatoes, sliced
1 onion, sliced
1 to 2 green peppers, sliced

salt and pepper to taste
1/4 c. butter, sliced
salad seasoning to taste

Combine potatoes, onion and green peppers in a grill-safe pan; sprinkle with salt and pepper to taste. Sprinkle with butter slices and salad seasoning. Grill until tender. Serves 6 to 8.

Citrus-Grilled Pork Tenderloin

Jo Ann

1-lb. pork tenderloin, sliced
  3/4-inch thick
1/2 t. pepper

2/3 c. orange marmalade
1/4 c. fresh mint, chopped
1/4 c. soy sauce

4 cloves garlic, minced

Sprinkle pork slices with pepper. Combine remaining ingredients; stir well. Brush over pork, reserving remaining marmalade mixture. Place pork on a lightly greased grill over high heat; grill for 3 minutes per side, or until no longer pink. Baste frequently with reserved marmalade mixture. Place marmalade mixture in a saucepan and bring to a boil over medium heat; cook for one minute. Drizzle over pork. Serves 4.

Zesty Grilled Pork Chops

Irene Robinson, Cincinnati, OH

3/4 c. soy sauce
1/4 c. lemon juice

1 T. chili sauce
1 T. brown sugar, packed

1/4 t. garlic powder
6 pork chops

Combine all ingredients except pork chops in a large plastic zipping bag; mix well. Reserve and refrigerate 1/4 cup of mixture for basting. Place pork chops in bag; shake to coat. Refrigerate 3 hours or overnight. Drain and discard marinade. Grill chops, covered, for 4 minutes; turn and baste with reserved mixture. Grill for 4 to 7 minutes, until juices run clear. Serves 6.

Quick tip

Dining outdoors on a hot, humid day? Keep salt free-flowing by placing a few dry grains of rice in the shaker.

Zesty Grilled Pork Chops

Quick tip

Need a quick table decoration? Fill Mason jars with coarse salt, then tuck in a votive. The salt crystals will sparkle in the flickering light...perfect for casual suppers.

Grilled Meatloaf Sandwiches

Ultimate Grilled Cheese Sandwiches

Gladys Kielar, Whitehouse, OH

8 slices white bread
8 slices American cheese
8 t. margarine, softened

4 t. grated Parmesan cheese,
 divided

Assemble bread and cheese to make 4 sandwiches, enclosing 2 slices cheese in each. Spread outside of sandwiches with margarine; place on an ungreased baking sheet. Bake, uncovered, at 400 degrees for 8 minutes. Sprinkle with half of the Parmesan cheese. Flip sandwiches; sprinkle with remaining Parmesan. Return to oven for 6 to 8 minutes, until golden. Makes 4 servings.

Grilled Meatloaf Sandwiches

Darrell Lawry, Kissimmee, FL

4 thick slices cooked meatloaf
3 T. oil, divided

8 slices sourdough bread, divided
4 t. coarse mustard

4 t. catsup
4 slices Monterey Jack cheese

In a skillet over medium heat, brown meatloaf slices on both sides in one tablespoon oil. Spread 4 slices bread with mustard; spread remaining bread with catsup. Arrange meatloaf on mustard-covered bread slices; top with cheese. Top with catsup-covered slices. Heat remaining oil in a skillet over medium heat. Cook sandwiches on both sides, until golden and cheese is melted. Serves 4.

Herb-Grilled Steak

Carla Pindell, Hilliard, OH

3 to 4-lb. beef sirloin or
   porterhouse steak,
   1 to 1-1/2 inches thick
1 t. onion salt
1/2 c. vinegar
1/4 c. oil
1/4 t. dried thyme
1/4 t. dried tarragon
1/4 t. dried dill weed
1/4 t. dried sage

Rub both sides of steak with onion salt; place in a shallow container and set aside. Combine remaining ingredients and pour over steak. Marinate at least one hour, turning occasionally. Grill or broil steak about 6 inches from heat, 15 to 20 minutes on each side, brushing frequently with herb marinade. Serves 6 to 8.

Grilled Garlic-Stuffed Steaks

Tricia Schreier, San Jose, CA

1 T. olive oil
1/4 c. garlic, chopped
1/2 c. green onion,
   chopped
1/4 t. pepper
2 boneless beef top loin
   steaks, cut 2 inches thick

Heat oil in a skillet; add garlic and sauté for 4 to 5 minutes, until tender. Sprinkle in onion; continue to cook for 4 to 5 more minutes, until tender. Sprinkle with pepper and set aside. Cut a pocket in each steak; start 1/2 inch from one long side of steak and cut horizontally through the center of the steak to within 1/2 inch of other side. Spread half of garlic mixture inside each steak pocket; secure opening with a metal skewer. Grill, covered, for 22 to 24 minutes or to desired doneness, turning occasionally. Slice steaks crosswise 1/2-inch thick. Serves 6.

Triple Garlic Steak Sandwiches

Alicia Van Duyne, Braidwood, IL

1 lb. sliced mushrooms
1 onion, thinly sliced
1 green pepper, thinly
   sliced
2 t. extra-virgin olive oil
2 t. garlic powder
6 thin-cut boneless beef
   ribeye steaks or sliced
   beef sandwich steaks
2 t. garlic salt
6 slices mozzarella cheese
1/2 c. butter, softened
3 T. garlic, pressed
6 hard rolls, split
Optional: favorite steak
   sauce

Place vegetables on a long piece of heavy-duty aluminum foil. Sprinkle with olive oil and garlic powder. Place foil on grate over medium-high heat. Grill until vegetables are tender, about 10 to 12 minutes; remove from grill and set aside. Add steaks to grill and sprinkle with garlic salt. Cook to desired doneness, about 2 to 3 minutes per side. Remove from grill; top with cheese slices and keep warm. Blend butter and pressed garlic in a small bowl. Spread butter mixture over cut sides of rolls. Grill rolls cut-side down until toasted. To serve, top each roll with a steak, a spoonful of vegetable mixture and some steak sauce, if desired. Serves 6.

Triple Garlic Steak Sandwiches

Grilled Salami Pizza Sandwiches

Grilled Salami Pizza Sandwiches

Marion Gene, Daytona, FL

2/3 c. pizza sauce
8 slices bread
4 slices deli salami

4 slices American cheese
garlic salt to taste
1 T. butter, softened

Spread pizza sauce on one side of 4 bread slices. Top each bread slice with one salami slice and one cheese slice; sprinkle with garlic salt. Top with remaining bread slices. Generously butter top and bottom of sandwiches. Heat a skillet over medium heat; add sandwiches and cook on both sides until bread is toasted and cheese is melted. Makes 4 servings.

Grilled Western Chicken Sandwich

Thomas Campbell, Hopkins, MN

4 boneless, skinless
chicken breasts
12-oz. bottle western salad
dressing
1 T. pepper

4 kaiser onion rolls, split
and toasted
Garnish: 4 lettuce leaves,
4 thick slices tomato

Place chicken breasts, salad dressing and pepper in a gallon-size plastic zipping bag. Seal bag; shake gently to coat chicken. Refrigerate for 3 hours to overnight. Heat a grill to medium-high, about 350 degrees. Remove chicken from bag; discard marinade. Grill chicken until cooked through and chicken juices run clear when pierced. Place each piece of chicken on a toasted bun bottom; top with lettuce, tomato and top of bun. Makes 4 servings.

Grilled Salmon BLTs

Edie DeSpain, Logan, UT

1/3 c. mayonnaise
2 t. fresh dill, chopped
1 t. lemon zest
4 1-inch-thick salmon
fillets
1/4 t. salt
1/8 t. pepper

8 1/2-inch slices
country-style bread
4 romaine lettuce leaves
2 tomatoes, sliced
6 slices bacon, crisply
cooked and halved

Stir together mayonnaise, dill and zest; set aside. Sprinkle salmon with salt and pepper; place skin-side down on a lightly greased hot grill. Cook, covered, about 10 to 12 minutes without turning, until cooked through. Slide a thin metal spatula between salmon and skin; lift salmon and transfer to plate. Discard skin. Arrange bread slices on grill; cook until lightly toasted on both sides. Spread mayonnaise mixture on one side of 4 toasted bread slices. Top each with one lettuce leaf, 2 tomato slices, one salmon fillet, 3 slices bacon and remaining bread slice. Makes 4 servings.

Quick tip

Let the kids invite a special friend or two home on a cookout night. Keep it simple with Grilled Salami Pizza Sandwiches and a crisp salad. A great way to get to know your children's playmates!

Herb-Buttered Grilled Corn

Dale Duncan, Waterloo, IA

6 ears corn	2 t. fresh basil, minced
1/3 c. butter, softened	2 t. fresh oregano, minced

Pull back husks of corn, leaving them attached. Remove and discard silk; replace husks around corn. Place corn in a large stockpot; fill with water to cover. Soak 20 minutes; drain. Pull back husks of corn; set aside. Blend butter with herbs and brush evenly over corn; replace husks. Grill corn over medium-high heat, covered, about 15 minutes, until corn is tender. Serves 6.

Grilled Fresh Veggie Combo

Jennifer Weber, Williamsville, NY

1 zucchini, thinly sliced	olive oil to taste
1 yellow squash, thinly sliced	chopped fresh basil, oregano, rosemary or parsley to taste
1 red onion, thinly sliced	
1 T. garlic, minced	

Use a vegetable grill basket or a length of heavy-duty aluminum foil with the sides rolled up to shape into a bowl. Coat inside of basket or foil with non-stick vegetable spray; fill with vegetables. Place on a grill preheated to medium heat. Cook until vegetables are crisp-tender. Remove from grill; transfer vegetables to a serving dish. Lightly drizzle with oil; add desired chopped herbs and serve immediately. Serves 6.

Grilled Vegetable Salad

Jo Ann

1 ear corn, husked	1 c. couscous, cooked
16 spears asparagus, trimmed	6-oz. pkg. spring greens
16 green onions, trimmed	1/4 c. lemon juice
8 roma tomatoes, halved	1 t. Dijon mustard
1 bulb fennel, thinly sliced	salt and pepper to taste
1/2 c. plus 2 to 3 T. olive oil, divided	Garnish: chopped fresh basil, parsley and/or mint

Place all vegetables in a grill basket. Drizzle with 2 to 3 tablespoons oil; season with salt and pepper. Place basket on a grate over high heat. Cook until tender, about 5 to 10 minutes, turning occasionally. Remove grill basket from grill; cool. Slice corn kernels off cob; cut other vegetables into bite-size pieces. Combine all vegetables in a large salad bowl. Add couscous and greens. For vinaigrette, whisk together remaining olive oil, lemon juice, mustard and salt and pepper to taste. Add desired amount of vinaigrette to vegetable mixture; toss to mix. Garnish with herbs. Serves 4 to 6.

Quick tip

Homemade salt-free herb seasoning adds zesty flavor to all kinds of grilled veggies and meats. Combine a tablespoon each of dried oregano, basil and pepper, 1-1/2 teaspoons each of onion powder and thyme and a teaspoon of garlic powder. Fill a large shaker container to keep conveniently by the grill.

Grilled Fresh Veggie Combo

Grilled Sausage & Veggies

Grilled Sausage & Veggies

Vickie

1-1/2 lbs. green beans, trimmed
1 lb. redskin potatoes, quartered
1 to 2 sweet onions, sliced

1-1/2 lbs. smoked sausage, cut in
  1-inch pieces
1 t. salt

1 t. pepper
1 T. butter, sliced
1/2 c. water

Arrange beans, potatoes and onions on a large sheet of aluminum foil; top with sausage. Add salt and pepper; dot with butter. Bring up aluminum foil around ingredients; sprinkle with water and close tightly. Place packet on a hot grill; cook for 30 to 45 minutes, turning once, until sausage is browned and vegetables are tender. Serves 4.

Lemony Grilled Broccoli

Erin Brock, Charleston, WV

2-1/2 T. lemon juice
2 T. olive oil
1/4 t. salt

1/4 t. pepper
1 bunch broccoli, cut into spears
  and trimmed

3/4 c. grated Parmesan cheese

In a large bowl, whisk together lemon juice, oil, salt and pepper; add broccoli and toss to coat. Let stand for 30 minutes. Toss broccoli again; drain and discard marinade. Place cheese in a large plastic zipping bag. Add broccoli, a few pieces at a time; shake to coat. Grill broccoli, covered, on an oiled grate over medium heat for 8 to 10 minutes on each side, until crisp-tender. Serves 4 to 6.

Hawaiian Grilled Pork Chops

Jan Stafford, Trenton, GA

20-oz. can pineapple slices
6 pork chops
1/2 c. soy sauce
1/3 c. oil

1/4 c. onion, minced
1 clove garlic, minced
1 T. brown sugar, packed

Drain pineapple, reserving 1/4 cup juice; set aside. Place pork chops in a large shallow dish. Combine reserved pineapple juice, soy sauce, oil, onion, garlic and brown sugar; mixing well. Pour over pork chops; cover and marinate in refrigerator for 30 minutes to 2 hours. Remove pork chops, reserving marinade. In a saucepan, bring marinade to a boil; boil for 3 minutes. Grill over medium heat for 4 to 5 minutes per side, turning frequently and basting with marinade. Top each pork chop with a pineapple slice during the last 5 minutes of grilling. Makes 6 servings.

Polynesian Ginger Spareribs

Jill Valentine, Jackson, TN

1/2 c. soy sauce
1/2 c. brown sugar, packed
1/2 c. green onions, chopped
1/4 c. catsup

2 cloves garlic, pressed
1 t. fresh ginger, peeled and grated
3 lbs. pork spareribs, cut into serving-size portions

In a microwave-safe dish, mix all ingredients except spareribs. Add spareribs; turn until well coated. Drain marinade into a bowl. Cover ribs with plastic wrap; let stand for 10 minutes. Microwave ribs on medium-high setting for 12 to 16 minutes. In a saucepan, bring marinade to a boil; boil for 3 minutes. Place ribs on an oiled grate over medium-high heat; brush with marinade. Grill for 8 to 10 minutes, turning and brushing once or twice with marinade. Serves 4 to 6.

Tangy Peach-Glazed Chicken

Kathleen Sturm, Corona, CA

3 lbs. chicken
1 c. peach jam or preserves
2 T. oil
1 T. plus 1 t. soy sauce
1 T. dry mustard

1 clove garlic, minced
1/4 t. cayenne pepper
1 t. salt
1/2 t. pepper

Place chicken on an oiled grate over medium-high heat. Grill for 30 to 40 minutes turning occasionally. Meanwhile, combine remaining ingredients in a bowl; mix well. Brush peach mixture generously over chicken during last 10 minutes of cooking. Grill until chicken juices run clear when pierced. Makes 8 servings.

Quick tip

For the most mouthwatering marinated chops and steaks, pat the meat dry with a paper towel after draining off the marinade. Then sprinkle on any seasonings before placing it on the hot grill.

Tangy Peach–Glazed Chicken

Quick tip

Use a grill basket to cook small pieces of meat, fish and veggies...they won't fall through the grate and are much easier to turn for even cooking.

Haddock & Creamy Dill Sauce

Ginger-Lime Grilled Salmon

Jo Ann

2 T. butter, melted
2 T. fresh ginger, peeled and
  minced

2 T. lime zest
1 T. lime juice
1/2 t. salt

1/2 t. pepper
2 lbs. salmon fillets, 1-inch thick
Garnish: lime wedges

In a small bowl, combine all ingredients except salmon and garnish. Rub mixture over salmon fillets. Place fish on a lightly oiled grate over medium-high heat. Cover and grill about 5 minutes on each side, until fish flakes easily with a fork. Garnish with lime wedges. Serves 4 to 6.

Haddock & Creamy Dill Sauce

Claudia Keller, Carrollton, GA

1 lb. haddock fillets
1 T. olive oil
salt and pepper to taste

1/2 c. sour cream
1 T. fresh dill, chopped
1 t. lemon juice

Garnish: fresh dill sprigs, thinly
  sliced lemon

Brush fish with oil; season with salt and pepper. Place on a lightly oiled grate over medium heat. Grill for about 4 minutes on each side, turning once, until fish flakes easily with a fork. Stir together remaining ingredients except garnish. Serve fillets topped with sauce; garnish as desired. Serves 4.

Grilled Lemon-Herb Chicken

Betty Flanigan, Greensboro, NC

4 T. lemon juice
2 T. dry white wine or
    fat-free chicken broth
1 T. olive oil
salt and lemon pepper to
    taste

2 T. fresh lemon thyme or
    rosemary, chopped
4 boneless, skinless
    chicken breasts

Whisk together all ingredients except chicken. Spray a grill or broiler pan with non-stick vegetable spray; preheat. Grill or broil chicken until juices run clear, brushing several times with lemon mixture. Makes 4 servings.

Grilled Lemon Turkey

Jenny Bishoff, Mountain Lake Park, MD

1/4 c. olive oil
1/4 c. lemon juice
1/4 c. water
1 T. fresh rosemary,
    chopped, or 1 t. dried
    rosemary

1 to 2 t. lemon pepper
    seasoning
1 t. chicken bouillon
    granules
4 to 6 turkey cutlets

In a one-gallon plastic zipping bag, mix all ingredients except turkey; squeeze bag to mix. Add turkey to bag; seal. Refrigerate 4 hours to overnight, turning occasionally. Drain, discarding marinade. Grill turkey over medium heat about 10 to 15 minutes, turning once, until juices run clear. Serves 4 to 6.

Grilled Chicken Salad with Apple Dressing

Inez Rice, Marion, OH

1/2 c. apple juice
1 c. apple, peeled, cored
    and chopped
1 T. cider vinegar
1 t. cornstarch
1 lb. mixed salad greens
1/4 c. sliced almonds,
    toasted

1/2 c. shredded Cheddar
    cheese
1/2 c. red pepper, sliced
3/4 c. crumbled blue
    cheese
4 12-oz. boneless, skinless
    chicken breasts, grilled

Combine apple juice, apple, vinegar and cornstarch. Heat mixture over medium heat until mixture thickens. Cool in refrigerator. Tear salad greens and divide among 4 plates. On each plate, arrange almonds, Cheddar cheese, red pepper, blue cheese and chicken. Top with apple dressing. Makes 4 servings.

Grilled Chicken Salad with Apple Dressing

Mustard & Herb Strip Steak

Quick tip

Is it time to cook? If you can hold your hand comfortably 5 inches over the coals: 5 to 6 seconds = low heat, or 250 to 300 degrees, 4 seconds = medium heat, or 350 to 400 degrees, 2 seconds = high heat, or 400 to 450 degrees.

Gwen's Pit Beef

Gwen Stutler, Emporia, KS

1 T. dried oregano
1 T. dried thyme
1 T. garlic powder

1 T. lemon pepper
1 T. salt
1 T. pepper

3 to 4-lb. beef top round or eye
round roast

Combine spices in a small bowl. Pierce roast all over with a fork; rub and pat spice mixture all over roast. Preheat grill to highest setting. Place roast on an oiled grate. Cover and cook for about 25 to 35 minutes, turning every 7 minutes, until blackened on all sides. Use a meat thermometer inserted into center of roast, 140 degrees for rare, 145 degrees for medium-rare, 160 degrees for medium or 170 degrees for well-done. Remove from heat; let stand for 10 minutes. Slice thinly. Makes 6 to 8 servings.

Mustard & Herb Strip Steak

Dale Duncan, Waterloo, IA

2 to 3 cloves garlic, pressed
2 t. water
2 T. Dijon mustard

1 t. dried basil
1/2 t. dried thyme
1/2 t. pepper

2 8-oz. beef strip steaks or top loin
steaks, 3/4-inch thick
salt to taste

Combine garlic and water in a microwave-safe glass measuring cup. Microwave on high setting for 30 seconds. Stir in mustard, herbs and pepper. Brush mixture over both sides of steaks. Place steaks on an oiled grate over medium heat. Cover and grill to desired doneness, 11 minutes for medium-rare or 14 minutes for medium, turning occasionally. Season steaks with salt, as desired. Slice steaks crosswise into thick slices. Serves 2 to 4.

Mom's Best Burgers

Jacqueline Kurtz, Wernersville, PA

2 lbs. ground beef
1 onion, chopped
1/2 c. Italian-flavored dry
   bread crumbs

1/3 c. teriyaki sauce
1 T. grated Parmesan cheese
1 t. dried basil
1 t. salt

1 t. pepper
6 onion rolls, split
6 slices Cheddar cheese

In a large bowl, combine all ingredients except rolls and cheese. Mix well and form into 6 patties. Grill over medium-high heat to desired doneness, about 5 to 7 minutes on each side. Serve burgers on rolls, topped with cheese. Makes 6 servings.

Spicy Turkey Burgers

Louise Gilbert, British Columbia, Canada

1 lb. ground turkey
1/3 c. quick-cooking oats,
   uncooked
1/2 c. catsup

1 T. vinegar
1 T. Worcestershire sauce
2 cloves garlic, minced
1/4 to 1/2 t. red pepper flakes

1/4 t. hot pepper sauce
1/4 t. pepper
4 hamburger buns, split

Combine turkey and oats in a large bowl; set aside. In a small bowl, mix together remaining ingredients except buns. Add half of catsup mixture to turkey mixture; blend thoroughly. Form into 4 patties. Grill burgers over medium-high heat for 5 to 7 minutes; turn over. Baste with remaining sauce and grill another 5 to 7 minutes, to desired doneness. Serve burgers on buns. Makes 4 servings.

Mom's Best Burgers

🥄🍴🔪 *Quick tip*

Delicious burgers begin with ground beef chuck labeled as 80/20. A little fat in the beef adds flavor...there's no need to purchase expensive ground sirloin.

Grilled Jumbo Shrimp

Grilled Jumbo Shrimp

Lucy Lemen, Merrimack, NH

1/4 c. soy sauce
1 c. orange juice
1/4 c. olive oil
4 T. sugar
3 cloves garlic, minced
1 T. fresh ginger,
  peeled and finely
  chopped

1 T. lemon zest
2 lbs. uncooked jumbo
  shrimp, peeled
  and cleaned

In a small bowl, whisk together soy sauce, orange juice, olive oil, sugar, garlic, ginger and lemon zest. Add shrimp and marinate in refrigerator for at least one hour, stirring occasionally. Drain marinade; bring to a boil in a saucepan for 3 minutes. Thread shrimp onto skewers and grill about 2 minutes on each side, basting occasionally with marinade. Serves 6.

Grilled Salmon Salad

Sandy Thomas, Witchita, KS

10 to 12-oz. salmon fillet
1/2 c. lime juice
pepper to taste
4 c. spinach, torn
1 c. sweetened dried
  cranberries

1 c. crumbled blue cheese
1 c. sugared walnuts
1 tomato, sliced
vinaigrette or blue cheese
  salad dressing to taste

Dip salmon in lime juice on both sides; sprinkle with pepper. Grill over medium-high heat for 4 to 5 minutes per side, until fish flakes easily. Divide remaining ingredients except salad dressing among salad plates. Slice salmon; place over salads. Drizzle with desired amount of salad dressing. Serves 2.

Grilled Corn & Shrimp Salad

Nancy Fisher, Macon, GA

2 ears corn, husked
1 t. chili sauce
1/2 t. ground cumin
1/2 t. salt
1/4 t. pepper
2 lbs. uncooked large
  shrimp, peeled and
  cleaned
3 T. olive oil
2 to 3 tomatoes, cut into
  thin wedges

1/2 cucumber, halved
  lengthwise and thinly
  sliced
8 c. spring mix greens
1 avocado, pitted, peeled
  and thinly sliced
Asian sesame salad
  dressing to taste
Garnish: 2 T. fresh mint,
  thinly sliced

Grilled or broil corn for about 5 minutes, until lightly browned. Cool; slice off kernels and set aside. Stir together chili sauce, cumin, salt and pepper in a large bowl. Add shrimp; toss to coat. Heat oil in a large skillet over high heat. Add shrimp; sauté until no longer pink, about 3 minutes. Cool. In a bowl, combine shrimp, corn, tomatoes and cucumber; chill. At serving time, arrange greens on a serving platter. Top with shrimp mixture and avocado. Drizzle with dressing; sprinkle with mint. Makes 8 to 10 servings.

Grilled to Perfection

Grilled Fresh Summer Pizza

Sonia Daily, Rochester, MI

2 12-inch pre-baked
   Italian pizza crusts
6-1/2 oz. container garlic
   & herb spreadable cream
   cheese
2 roma tomatoes, thinly
   sliced

1/2 red onion, chopped
8 slices bacon, crisply
   cooked and crumbled
olive oil to taste
8-oz. pkg. shredded
   mozzarella cheese
1/2 c. fresh basil, chopped

Preheat grill to medium heat. Spread cream cheese
over pizza crusts. Top with tomatoes, onion and bacon.
Drizzle with oil and sprinkle with mozzarella cheese.
Place pizzas on grill and reduce to low heat. Cover and
cook for 5 to 8 minutes, until crusts are golden and
cheese is melted. Remove from grill; top with basil and
cut into wedges. Makes 12 servings.

Grilled BBQ Chicken Pizza

Phyllis Wittig, Quartz Hill, CA

13.8-oz. tube refrigerated
   pizza dough
1 c. barbecue sauce
2 boneless, skinless
   chicken breasts, cooked
   and cut into strips

8-oz. pkg. shredded
   mozzarella cheese
1/2 c. green onion,
   chopped

Spray a baking sheet with non-stick vegetable spray;
lay out dough according to package directions. Spread
sauce over dough; arrange cooked chicken strips on top.
Sprinkle with shredded cheese. Spray cold grill with
non-stick vegetable spray; preheat grill. Carefully lift
dough off baking sheet onto grill; grill over low heat for
10 minutes. Use a spatula to remove pizza from grill;
sprinkle with green onion. Slice into squares. Serves 4.

Grilled Grecian Salad Pizza

Lisa Kastning, Marysville, WA

3 T. olive oil, divided
4 cloves garlic, minced
3 c. romaine lettuce,
   shredded
1 T. lemon juice
2 12-inch pre-baked
   Italian pizza crusts
2 to 3 tomatoes, thinly
   sliced

1-1/2 c. crumbled feta
   cheese
6 to 8 pepperoncini,
   chopped
1 c. chopped black olives
2 T. fresh oregano, minced
cracked pepper to taste

Heat 1-1/2 tablespoons olive oil in a large skillet over
medium heat. Add garlic; sauté until lightly golden. Add
lettuce and lemon juice to skillet; stir quickly, just until
lettuce is wilted. Brush remaining olive oil over pizza
crusts. Top with tomatoes, lettuce mixture and remaining
ingredients. Place pizzas on grill over medium-high heat;
close cover. Cook until crusts are golden, vegetables are
heated through and cheese is beginning to melt. Cut into
wedges. Makes 12 to 16 servings.

 Quick side

Grill up a salad! Choose small heads
of romaine or slice larger ones in half
lengthwise; don't separate the leaves. Rinse,
pat dry and spritz with olive oil. Grill over
high heat for 2 to 3 minutes per side, until
lightly wilted and golden. Serve lettuce
drizzled with balsamic vinaigrette.

Grilled Fresh Summer Pizza

Pork & Peach Kabobs

Pork & Peach Kabobs

Ed Smulski, Lyons, IL

2 peaches, halved, pitted
  and cut into 6 wedges
1 sweet onion, cut into
  6 wedges
1-1/2 lbs. pork tenderloin,
  cut into 18 to 20 cubes

6 skewers
3/4 c. honey barbecue
  sauce
Optional: cooked brown
  rice

Cut peach and onion wedges crosswise in half. Thread peach, onion and pork pieces alternately onto skewers, leaving some space in between for even grilling. Grill skewers over medium-high heat for 15 minutes, or until pork juices run clear, turning skewers occasionally. Brush with barbecue sauce during the last 5 minutes. Serve with cooked rice, if desired. Makes 6 servings.

Grilled Ham & Pineapple

Sharon Dennison, Floyds Knobs, IN

1 fresh pineapple
3 T. honey
1/4 c. mustard
1/4 c. pineapple juice
2 T. brown sugar, packed

1/2 t. prepared horseradish
1/8 t. salt
1-1/2 to 2-lb. ham steak,
  1-inch thick

Remove top of pineapple but do not peel. Cut pineapple lengthwise into 8 wedges. Place wedges in a pan and brush with honey. Cover and refrigerate for one hour, turning occasionally. Place pineapple wedges skin-side down on an oiled grate over medium-high heat. Grill for 20 minutes, or until hot. Meanwhile, for sauce, mix together remaining ingredients except ham. Cut ham steak into serving-size pieces, if desired. Grill ham, brushing often with sauce, until glazed and heated through. Serve ham with pineapple and remaining sauce for drizzling. Serves 4 to 6.

Hawaiian Bar-B-Que Burgers

Cindy McKinnon, El Dorado, AR

2 lbs. ground beef
2 t. Worcestershire sauce
1/2 c. favorite barbecue
  sauce
1/2 c. pineapple preserves
1 T. brown sugar, packed

20-oz. can sliced
  pineapple, drained
6 to 8 hamburger buns,
  split
Optional: lettuce leaves,
  cheese slices

Combine beef and Worcestershire sauce in a large bowl. Mix thoroughly; form into 6 to 8 patties and set aside. Combine barbecue sauce, preserves and brown sugar in a small saucepan. Bring to a boil over medium heat, stirring frequently. Remove from heat. Brush patties with sauce mixture and place on a grill over medium heat. Cook to desired doneness, 5 to 7 minutes on each side, brushing with sauce mixture after each turn. Meanwhile, brush pineapple slices with sauce mixture and add to grill; cook for 2 minutes on each side. Grill buns. Top each bun with a burger, a pineapple slice, a lettuce leaf, some extra sauce mixture and a cheese slice, if desired. Makes 6 to 8 servings.

Quick tip

Safety first! Be sure to place grilled meat on a clean plate, never on a plate that previously held raw meat.

Grilled Parmesan Bread

Nancy Molldrem, Eau Claire, WI

1/4 c. butter, softened   1/2 c. grated Parmesan cheese   6 slices French bread, 1 inch thick

Blend butter and cheese in a small bowl. Spread mixture on both sides of bread slices. Place on a grill over medium heat. Toast until golden, about 3 minutes on each side. Serves 6.

Grilled Pepperoni Log

Lori Rosenberg, University Heights, OH

16-oz. loaf frozen bread dough,   4-oz. pkg. sliced pepperoni   1/4 c. grated Parmesan cheese
  thawed   1 c. shredded mozzarella cheese   1-1/2 t. Italian seasoning

Preheat grill until hot, about 375 degrees. On a lightly floured surface, roll out thawed bread dough into a 13"x9" rectangle. Arrange pepperoni and cheeses evenly over dough. Sprinkle with seasoning. Roll up dough jelly-roll style, starting on one long edge; pinch seam to seal. Place dough seam-side down on grate over indirect heat. Cook for 20 minutes on each side. Slice to serve. Makes 12 to 14 servings.

Grilled Parmesan Bread

Bacon-Wrapped BBQ Chicken

Bacon-Wrapped BBQ Chicken

Nicole Culver, La Fontaine, IN

18-oz. bottle favorite
  barbecue sauce, divided
2 T. brown sugar, packed
onion powder to taste

4 to 6 boneless, skinless
  chicken breasts
1/2 to 1 lb. bacon

In a saucepan over low heat, combine sauce, brown sugar and onion powder. Simmer for 30 minutes, stirring occasionally. Meanwhile, wrap chicken breasts with one to 2 slices bacon each; secure with wooden toothpicks. Set aside 3/4 cup of sauce mixture. Brush remaining sauce mixture over chicken. Place chicken on an oiled grate over medium-high heat. Grill for 30 minutes, turning occasionally, until nearly done. Brush chicken well with reserved sauce mixture. Cook until chicken juices run clear and sauce is caramelized. Serves 4 to 6.

Barb's Teriyaki Sauce

Barb Rudyk, Alberta, Canada

1/2 c. light or regular soy
  sauce
3/4 to 1 c. brown sugar,
  packed
3/4 c. water

1 T. cornstarch
1/4 t. garlic powder
1/8 t. ground ginger

Combine all ingredients in a saucepan; whisk to mix well. Bring to a boil over medium-high heat, stirring constantly, until mixture boils and thickens slightly. Cool to room temperature. To use, brush over chicken when grilling or baking. Makes 1-1/2 cups sauce.

Tangy Apple BBQ Sauce

Jonathan Bastian, Mifflinburg, PA

1 c. catsup
1/2 c. brown sugar, packed
1/4 c. honey
1/4 c. molasses
1/4 c. Worcestershire sauce
1/2 t. pepper

1/4 t. smoke-flavored
  cooking sauce
1/8 t. chili powder
1 apple, peeled, cored and
  finely diced

Combine all ingredients in a saucepan over medium heat. Simmer, stirring occasionally, until thickened. Serve with grilled burgers or steak. Makes 2 cups.

Quick tip

A ridged cast-iron grill skillet is oh-so handy for grilling on your stovetop whenever it's too cold or rainy to use the grill outdoors.

Backyard Cheddar BBQ Burgers

Brandi Bryant, Baton Rouge, LA

1 lb. ground beef chuck
1-oz. pkg. ranch salad dressing
  mix

1 t. olive oil
1 c. shredded sharp Cheddar
  cheese

favorite barbecue sauce to taste
10 slices Texas toast
Garnish: favorite condiments

Mix together beef, salad dressing mix and oil in a large bowl. Form into 5 patties. Place a generous pinch of cheese into the center of each patty. Fold in and reshape patties until cheese is hidden inside. Grill burgers over medium heat for 20 minutes; turn. Brush burgers with barbecue sauce and grill for 5 more minutes, until sizzling. Serve burgers on Texas toast, topped with desired condiments. Makes 5 servings.

Caramelized Onion Burgers

Nancy Girard, Chesapeake, VA

1 lb. ground beef
1/4 c. fresh parsley, chopped
2 T. tomato paste
2 t. Worcestershire sauce

1/2 t. salt
1/4 t. pepper
4 hamburger buns, split and
  toasted

Optional: lettuce leaves, tomato
  slices

Prepare Caramelized Onion Topping; keep warm. Combine beef, parsley, tomato paste, Worcestershire sauce, salt and pepper. Form into 4 patties. Grill over medium heat to desired doneness, 6 to 8 minutes on each side. Serve burgers on buns, topped with spoonfuls of Caramelized Onion Topping and, if desired, lettuce and tomato. Makes 4 servings.

Carmelized Onion Topping:

2 T. olive oil
4 onions, sliced

2 t. sugar
1/4 c. water

1 T. balsamic vinegar
1/4 t. salt

Heat olive oil in a skillet over low heat. Add onions and sprinkle with sugar. Cook over low heat for 20 to 25 minutes, stirring often, until onions are carmelized and golden. Stir in water, vinegar and salt. Serve warm.

🥄🍴🔪 *Quick tip*

Put a new spin on burgers! Swap out the same ol' buns with different types of bread like English muffins, Italian ciabatta or sliced French bread. Pita rounds make sandwiches that are easier for littler hands to hold.

Backyard Cheddar BBQ Burgers

Black Bean Turkey Burgers

Pesto-Brie Grilled Chicken

Brenda Schlosser, Brighton, CO

4 boneless, skinless
   chicken breasts
1/4 c. basil pesto sauce

4 slices brie cheese,
   1/4-inch thick
salt and pepper to taste

Place chicken on an oiled grate over medium-high heat. Grill for 3 to 5 minutes; turn chicken over. Spread each piece with one tablespoon pesto and top with a cheese slice. Cover; continue cooking for 3 to 5 minutes, until cheese is melted and chicken juices run clear. Serves 4.

Grilled Italiano Spread

Barb Bargdill, Gooseberry Patch

8-oz. pkg. Neufchâtel
   cheese
1/4 c. basil pesto sauce
1 roma tomato, chopped

1/4 c. finely shredded
   Italian-blend cheese
shredded wheat crackers

Unwrap Neufchâtel cheese and place on a piece of heavy-duty aluminum foil. Top with pesto, tomato and shredded cheese. Place foil on grate over medium heat. Cover and grill for 8 to 10 minutes, until shredded cheese is melted and Neufchâtel cheese is softened but still holds its shape. Serve warm with crackers. Serves 10 to 12.

Black Bean Turkey Burgers

Amy Hunt, Traphill, NC

1-1/4 lbs. ground turkey
3/4 c. canned black beans,
   drained, rinsed and
   lightly mashed
1 c. tortilla chips, crushed

1 T. chili powder
1 T. ground cumin
salt and pepper to taste
6 hamburger buns, split

In a large bowl, combine turkey, beans, tortilla chips and seasonings. Mix well with your hands and form into 6 patties. Grill over medium-high heat for 6 to 8 minutes per side. Serve burgers on buns, topped with a scoop of Avocado & Onion Slaw. Makes 6 servings.

Avocado & Onion Slaw:

3 T. mayonnaise
1 T. vinegar
1/4 t. salt

1 avocado, halved, pitted
   and cubed
1/2 c. onion, thinly sliced

Mix together mayonnaise, vinegar and salt until well combined. Stir in avocado and onion.

Puddie's Peel & Eat Shrimp

Cris Goode, Mooresville, IN

1 T. seasoned salt
1 T. seafood seasoning

1 T. chili powder
1 t. canola oil

12-oz. pkg. frozen uncooked
  jumbo shrimp, thawed and
  cleaned

In a large bowl, mix seasonings and oil. Add shrimp and toss to coat; let stand for 20 minutes. Drain, discarding marinade. Place shrimp over medium-high heat. Cook for 5 to 10 minutes, until shrimp are pink. Peel and eat. Serves 4 to 6.

Fish-Ka-Bobs

Emily Martin, Ontario, Canada

1-1/2 lbs. salmon or halibut fillets,
  sliced into 1-1/2 inch thick strips
4 to 6 skewers

1 c. olive oil & vinegar salad
  dressing
2 T. lemon juice

1/4 c. fresh Italian parsley,
  chopped
1 T. fresh rosemary, chopped

If using salmon, remove and discard skin. Thread fish strips onto skewers. Place skewers in a shallow glass dish. Whisk together remaining ingredients in a bowl; drizzle over fish. Cover and refrigerate 30 minutes, turning skewers occasionally. Drain, discarding marinade. Place skewers on a lightly oiled grill over high heat. Cover and cook for 4 minutes per side, or until fish flakes easily with a fork. Makes 4 to 6 servings.

Quick tip

Soak wooden skewers in water for
30 minutes before adding meat and
veggies...skewers won't burn on the grill.
For even cooking, leave a little space
between the pieces on the skewers.

Fish-Ka-Bobs

Quick tip

Hickory, mesquite and applewood chips add wonderful smoky flavor to grilled foods. Just soak in water, drain and scatter onto hot coals.

Honey-Mustard Grilled Chicken

Grilled Chicken Salad

Larry Bodner, Dublin, OH

1 c. apple, peeled, cored and finely chopped
1/2 c. apple juice
1 T. cider vinegar

1 t. cornstarch
4 boneless, skinless chicken breasts
6-oz. pkg. mixed salad greens

1/2 c. red pepper, sliced
3/4 c. crumbled blue cheese
1/2 c. shredded Cheddar cheese
1/4 c. sliced almonds, toasted

Combine apple, juice, vinegar and cornstarch in a small saucepan over medium heat; cook and stir until thickened. Chill. Grill chicken breasts until juices run clear; let cool, then slice. Divide salad greens among 4 serving plates; top each with grilled chicken, red pepper and a sprinkling of cheeses and almonds. Drizzle with dressing and serve immediately. Makes 4 servings.

Honey-Mustard Grilled Chicken

Diana Chaney, Olathe, KS

2/3 c. Dijon mustard
1/2 c. honey

1/4 c. mayonnaise
2 t. red steak sauce

8 boneless, skinless chicken thighs

In a shallow bowl, whisk together all ingredients except chicken. Set aside 1/3 of mustard mixture for basting. Coat chicken in remaining mustard mixture. Grill chicken over medium heat for 18 to 20 minutes, turning occasionally, until chicken juices run clear. Brush occasionally with reserved mustard mixture during the last 10 minutes. Makes 8 servings.

Grilled Peaches

Lisa Ann Panzino DiNunzio, Vineland, NJ

4 peaches, halved and pitted
2 T. butter, melted

cinnamon to taste
8 scoops vanilla ice cream

Brush the cut side of each peach half lightly with butter. Place peaches cut-side down on a hot grill. Reduce heat and grill for 8 to 10 minutes, until tender. Remove to serving bowls. Sprinkle with cinnamon. Top with a scoop of ice cream. Serves 8.

Yummy Banana Boats

Jen Licon-Connor, Gooseberry Patch

4 bananas
1/2 c. semi-sweet chocolate chips

1/2 c. mini marshmallows
Optional: 1/2 c. chopped peanuts

For each banana, pull back one section of peel without removing it; cut out a wedge lengthwise in the banana. Fill with chocolate chips, marshmallows and peanuts, if using. Pat peel back into place; wrap banana in aluminum foil. Cook bananas in campfire coals or on a hot grill for 5 minutes, or until chocolate and marshmallows are melted. Bananas may also be baked at 350 degrees for 7 to 10 minutes. Let cool slightly before unwrapping. Makes 4 servings.

Grilled Pineapple Sundaes

Cheri Maxwell, Gulf Breeze, FL

1/2 c. brown sugar, packed
2 T. butter, melted
2 T. lemon juice
1 t. cinnamon
1 pineapple, peeled, cored and sliced 1-inch thick

Garnish: vanilla ice cream
Optional: toasted coconut, maraschino cherries

In a bowl, mix brown sugar, butter, lemon juice and cinnamon. Brush mixture over both sides of pineapple slices. Grill pineapple over high heat for about one minute on each side, until golden. Remove each slice to a dessert plate. Serve warm, topped with a scoop of ice cream and garnished as desired. Serves 4 to 6.

Grilled Pineapple Sundaes

Poor Man's Steak & Vegetables

Batter-Topped Chicken Pot Pie
Jill Moore, Newark, OH

9-inch pie crust
2 c. cooked chicken, chopped
15-oz. can mixed vegetables, drained
10-3/4 oz. can cream of chicken & herbs soup
salt and pepper to taste
1/2 c. all-purpose flour
1/2 c. butter, melted
1/2 c. milk

Press pie crust into a greased 9" glass pie plate and set aside. In a bowl, mix chicken, vegetables, soup, salt and pepper. Spoon mixture into crust and smooth out surface. Whisk together remaining ingredients to make a very thin batter. Pour batter over filling. Bake at 350 degrees for one hour, or until golden and bubbly. Makes 6 servings.

French Bread Sausage Pizza
Christine Gordon, Rapid City, SD

1 loaf French bread, halved lengthwise
15-oz. can pizza sauce
1 lb. ground pork sausage, browned and drained
3-1/2 oz. pkg. sliced pepperoni
8-oz. pkg. shredded mozzarella cheese

Place both halves of loaf on an ungreased baking sheet, cut-side up. Spread with pizza sauce; top with sausage, pepperoni and cheese. Bake at 350 degrees for 15 minutes, or until cheese is melted. Slice to serve. Makes 6 to 8 servings.

Poor Man's Steak & Vegetables
Cynthia Armstrong, Big Stone Gap, VA

6 ground beef patties
4 potatoes, peeled and cubed
3 carrots, peeled and diced
1 onion, quartered or sliced
salt and pepper to taste

Place patties in a greased 13"x9" baking pan. Evenly arrange vegetables over patties. Sprinkle with salt and pepper to taste. Bake, covered, at 400 degrees for 45 to 50 minutes, until beef is no longer pink and potatoes are tender. Serves 6.

Quick tip
Is dinner taking just a little longer than planned? Set out bowls of unshelled walnuts or peanuts for a quick appetizer that will keep tummies from rumbling.

Ripe Tomato Tart

Darlene Lohrman, Chicago, IL

9-inch pie crust
1-1/2 c. shredded
  mozzarella cheese,
  divided
4 roma tomatoes, cut into
  wedges
3/4 c. fresh basil, chopped

4 cloves garlic, minced
1/2 c. mayonnaise
1/2 c. grated Parmesan
  cheese
1/8 t. white pepper

Line an ungreased 9" tart pan with pie crust; press crust into fluted sides of pan and trim edges. Bake at 450 degrees for 5 to 7 minutes; remove from oven. Sprinkle with 1/2 cup mozzarella cheese; let cool on a wire rack. Combine remaining ingredients; mix well and fill crust. Reduce heat to 375 degrees; bake for about 20 minutes, until bubbly on top. Makes 6 servings.

Basil & Tomato Soup

Vickie

2 T. oil
1 onion, chopped
2 to 3 tomatoes, chopped
1-1/2 lbs. yellow squash,
  chopped

3 c. chicken broth
1 c. buttermilk
1/4 c. fresh basil, minced
Garnish: fresh basil sprigs

Heat oil in a skillet over medium heat. Sauté onion until tender, about 5 minutes. Add tomatoes and continue to cook for 5 minutes, or until tomatoes are soft. Stir in squash and chicken broth; bring to a boil. Reduce heat and simmer 15 minutes, or until squash is fork-tender. Working in batches, spoon mixture into a blender or food processor; purée with buttermilk until mixture is smooth. Sprinkle in basil; stir. Garnish servings with more fresh basil. Serves 6 to 8.

Mom's Corn Oysters

Susan Tyrie Logsdon, Bowling Green, KY

2 c. creamed or whole corn
2 eggs, beaten
1/2 c. cracker crumbs
1/2 c. all-purpose flour

1/2 t. baking powder
1 t. salt
1/4 t. pepper
oil for frying

Combine corn, eggs and cracker crumbs; set aside. Sift together flour, baking powder, salt and pepper; add to corn mixture and stir well. Heat a small amount of oil in a skillet over medium-high heat. Drop batter into oil by tablespoonfuls, flattening slightly. Pan-fry until golden, about 3 minutes, turning once. Drain on paper towels. Serves 4 to 6.

Quick tip

No peeking! When baking, every time the oven door is opened, the temperature drops 25 degrees.

Ripe Tomato Tart

Ham & Feta Cheese Omelet

Creamed Ham on Cornbread

Cara Lorenz, Olathe, CO

8-1/2 oz. pkg. corn muffin mix
1/3 c. milk
1 egg, beaten

2 T. butter
2 T. all-purpose flour
1/4 t. salt

1-1/2 c. milk
3/4 c. shredded Cheddar cheese
1-1/2 c. cooked ham, cubed

Combine muffin mix, milk and egg; mix well and pour into a greased 8"x8" baking pan. Bake at 400 degrees for 18 to 20 minutes. In a saucepan, melt butter over low heat. Stir in flour and salt. Slowly add milk, whisking until smooth. Bring to a boil; boil and stir for 2 minutes. Stir in cheese and ham; heat through. Cut cornbread into squares; top with creamed ham. Makes 6 servings.

Ham & Feta Cheese Omelet

Holly Jackson, Saint George, UT

2 eggs, beaten
1/4 c. crumbled feta cheese
1/4 c. cucumber, diced

2 T. green onion, chopped
1/4 c. cooked ham, cubed
salt and pepper to taste

Garnish: salsa

Combine all ingredients except salsa in a bowl; mix well. Pour into a lightly greased sauté pan or small skillet. Without stirring, cook over low heat until set. Fold over; transfer to serving plate. Serve with salsa. Makes one serving.

Simple Spinach Quiche

Diane Cohen, Breinigsville, PA

9-inch pie crust
2 eggs, beaten
1 c. milk

1/2 t. salt
1/4 t. pepper
1-1/2 c. shredded Cheddar cheese

1/2 c. grated Parmesan cheese
10-oz. pkg. frozen spinach, thawed
 and well drained

Arrange pie crust in a 9-inch pie plate; flute edges and set aside. In a bowl, whisk together eggs, milk, salt and pepper. Fold in cheeses and spinach; pour mixture into pie crust. Bake at 350 degrees for 45 minutes, or until knife inserted into center comes out clean. Cut into wedges; serve warm. Makes 8 servings.

Dinners-on-a-Dime

Lomo Saltado

Patti Chandler, Dacula, GA

3 to 4 T. oil, divided
4 to 5 potatoes, peeled and thinly sliced
2 lbs. beef flank steak, thinly sliced
salt and pepper to taste

2 tomatoes, diced
1 green pepper, sliced
1 onion, sliced
cooked rice

Heat 3 tablespoons oil in a large skillet over medium-high heat. Cook potatoes until golden; drain and set aside. Add beef and more oil, if necessary. Stir-fry until browned. Drain and remove from skillet; sprinkle with salt and pepper and set aside. Add tomatoes, green pepper and onion to skillet; stir-fry until crisp-tender. Return beef mixture and potatoes to skillet; stir until well blended. Serve with rice. Makes 4 servings.

Picnic Hot Dog Surprise

Chris Breen, Las Vegas, NV

1 lb. hot dogs, sliced 1/4-inch thick
1/2 c. shredded Cheddar cheese
2 eggs, hard-boiled, peeled and chopped
2 to 3 green onions, diced

3 T. chili sauce
2 T. pickle relish
1 t. mustard
1/2 t. garlic salt
8 hot dog buns, split

Mix together all ingredients except buns. Hollow out bun tops by pulling out a little of the bread; fill buns with hot dog mixture. Wrap each bun in aluminum foil. Place on a baking sheet and bake at 350 degrees for 10 to 12 minutes, until heated through. Buns may also be warmed on a campfire grate for 10 to 12 minutes, turning often so they don't burn. Makes 8 servings.

Tangy Watermelon Salad

Belva Conner, Hillsdale, IN

14 c. watermelon, cubed
1 red onion, halved and thinly sliced
1 c. green onions, chopped
3/4 c. orange juice
5 T. red wine vinegar
2 T. plus 1-1/2 t. honey
1 T. green pepper, finely chopped

1/2 t. salt
1/4 t. pepper
1/4 t. garlic powder
1/4 t. onion powder
1/4 t. dry mustard
3/4 c. oil

In a large bowl, combine watermelon and onion; set aside. In a small bowl, combine orange juice, vinegar, honey, green pepper and seasonings; slowly whisk in oil. Pour over watermelon mixture; toss gently. Cover and refrigerate for at least 2 hours. Serve with a slotted spoon. Makes about 10 servings.

Quick tip

Fresh eggs can safely be kept in the refrigerator for four to five weeks...go ahead and stock up when they're on sale.

Tangy Watermelon Salad

Breakfast Burritos

Quick tip

Egg dishes are a terrific way to use up tasty tidbits from the fridge...chopped veggies, deli meats and cheese. Warm ingredients briefly in the skillet before scrambling in the eggs.

Savory Breakfast Pancakes

Jessica Parker, Mulvane, KS

2 c. biscuit baking mix
1 c. milk
2 eggs, beaten
1/2 c. shredded mozzarella cheese

1/2 c. pepperoni, chopped
1/2 c. tomato, chopped
1/4 c. green pepper, chopped
2 t. Italian seasoning

Garnish: pizza sauce, grated
   Parmesan cheese

Stir together baking mix, milk and eggs until well blended; add remaining ingredients except garnish. Heat a lightly greased griddle over medium-high heat. Ladle batter by 1/4 cupfuls onto the griddle; cook until golden on both sides. Garnish with warmed pizza sauce and Parmesan cheese. Makes 15 pancakes.

Breakfast Burritos

Cherie White, Oklahoma City, OK

16-oz. pkg. ground pork sausage
8-oz. pkg. shredded Mexican-blend
   cheese

10-oz. can diced tomatoes with
   green chiles
5 eggs, beaten

8 10-inch flour tortillas

Brown sausage in a skillet; drain. In a bowl, combine sausage, cheese and tomatoes. Cook eggs in the skillet. Add eggs to sausage mixture and mix thoroughly. Divide mixture evenly among tortillas and roll tightly. Seal tortillas by cooking for one to 2 minutes on a hot griddle sprayed with non-stick vegetable spray. Makes 8 servings.

Italian Vegetable Soup

Phyllis Lakes, Hagerstown, Indiana

2 12-oz. pkgs. smoked
   pork sausage, sliced
26-oz. jar spaghetti sauce
2 14-oz. cans chicken
   broth

2 16-oz. pkgs. frozen
   Italian mixed vegetables
1 onion, diced
6 to 8 c. water

Combine all ingredients in a soup pot. Simmer over medium heat for 20 minutes, or until heated through. Makes 4 to 6 servings.

Unstuffed Green Pepper Soup

Peggy Cantrell, Okmulgee, OK

2 lbs. ground beef
2 10-3/4 oz. cans tomato
   soup
28-oz. can petite diced
   tomatoes
4-oz. can mushroom
   pieces, drained

2 c. green peppers, diced
1 c. onion, diced
1/4 c. brown sugar, packed
3 to 4 c. beef broth
2 c. cooked rice

In a stockpot over medium heat, brown ground beef; drain. Stir in soup, vegetables and brown sugar. Add desired amount of beef broth. Simmer, covered, until peppers and onion are tender, about 30 minutes. Stir in rice about 5 minutes before serving. Makes 8 servings.

Easy Potato-Cheddar Soup

Sara Downing, Whitehall, OH

10-3/4 oz. can cream of
   potato soup
10-3/4 oz. can Cheddar
   cheese soup
3 c. milk

1/4 t. salt
1/8 t. pepper
2 16-oz. cans whole
   potatoes, drained
   and diced

Combine soups, milk, salt and pepper in a large soup pot over medium heat; stir until blended. Add potatoes; simmer until hot and bubbly. Serves 6.

Unstuffed Green Pepper Soup

Golden Macaroni & Cheese

🍴 *Quick tip*

A full pantry is so reassuring! With pasta, rice, dried beans, favorite sauces, baking mixes and canned soups, veggies and fruit on hand, you're all set to stir up a satisfying meal anytime.

Barbecued Hot Dogs

Nancy McCann, Clearwater, FL

2 T. butter
1 onion, chopped
3/4 c. catsup
2 T. Worcestershire sauce

2 T. vinegar
2 T. sugar
1 t. mustard
1/2 t. paprika

1/8 t. pepper
1 lb. hot dogs, sliced lengthwise
Optional: hot dog buns

Melt butter in a skillet over medium heat. Add onion and cook until transparent, about 5 minutes. Stir in remaining ingredients except hot dogs. Reduce heat and simmer for 10 minutes. Place hot dogs in a lightly greased 13"x9" baking pan. Spoon sauce from skillet onto sliced hot dogs and cover with remaining sauce. Bake, uncovered, at 350 degrees for 30 minutes. Serve on buns, if desired. Serves 4 to 6.

Golden Macaroni & Cheese

Gail Harris, Fort Worth, TX

10-3/4 oz. can cream of mushroom
  soup
1/2 c. milk

1/2 t. mustard
1/8 t. pepper
3 c. elbow macaroni, cooked

2 c. shredded Cheddar cheese,
  divided
1 c. French fried onions

Blend soup, milk, mustard and pepper in a lightly greased 1-1/2 quart casserole dish. Stir in macaroni and 1-1/2 cups cheese. Bake, uncovered, at 350 degrees for 20 minutes. Top with remaining cheese and onions; bake 10 additional minutes. Serves 4.

Bratwurst & Potato Salad

Marsha Shoning, Woodward, OK

6 bratwurst
1/4 c. bacon drippings or oil
2 lbs. redskin potatoes, quartered
  and boiled

1 bunch green onions, thinly sliced
1/2 c. olive oil
3 T. white wine vinegar
2 T. German mustard

salt and pepper to taste
Optional: 1/8 t. sugar

Cook bratwurst according to package instructions; brown in bacon drippings or oil. Cut into one-inch pieces. Combine bratwurst, potatoes and onions in a large bowl; set aside. Mix together remaining ingredients; pour over bratwurst mixture and toss to coat. Refrigerate 7 to 8 hours, or overnight. Serves 6 to 8.

Speedy Goulash

Laura Witham, Anchorage, AK

1 lb. ground beef
1 onion
2 cloves garlic
1 T. Hungarian paprika

1/2 T. ground coriander
1/2 T. ground cumin
1/4 t. nutmeg
14-1/2 oz. can diced tomatoes

3 T. sour cream
salt and pepper to taste
8-oz. pkg. elbow macaroni, cooked

Brown ground beef in a large skillet over medium heat. While beef is cooking, grate onion and garlic directly into beef; add spices and mix well. When beef is just cooked, drain. Add tomatoes with juice; warm through. Stir in sour cream, salt, pepper and cooked macaroni; serve immediately. Serves 6.

Bratwurst & Potato Salad

Quick tip

A super-simple tip for cutting down on wasted food...include family members in planning menus, shopping for groceries and preparing meals. Picky eaters are much more likely to eat food that they've chosen and cooked themselves!

Rustic Kielbasa Skillet

Rustic Kielbasa Skillet
Pat Crandall, Rochester, NY

12 new redskin potatoes,
    quartered
1 to 2 onions, quartered
1 green pepper, diced
1 T. olive oil

3/4 c. chicken broth
2 T. soy sauce
1-1/2 lbs. Kielbasa sausage,
    sliced 1/2-inch thick

In a large skillet over medium heat, cook potatoes, onions and pepper in oil until potatoes are golden. Add broth and soy sauce; cook until potatoes and vegetables are fork-tender. Toss in Kielbasa and cook until heated through. Serves 3 to 4.

Sausage & Pepper Bake
Sherri White, Jacksonville, FL

1-lb. pkg. ground pork
    sausage
14-oz. can tomato sauce
14-1/2 oz. can diced
    tomatoes
1/2 c. green pepper,
    chopped

1/2 c. red pepper, chopped
1/4 c. dried, minced onion
1-1/3 c. water
salt and pepper to taste
1 c. instant rice, uncooked

Brown sausage in a skillet over medium heat; drain. Add remaining ingredients except rice. Simmer for about 15 minutes. When mixture boils, stir in uncooked rice. Remove from heat; cover and let stand for about 10 minutes. Stir before serving. Serves 6.

Pepperoni Noodle Pizza
Gretchen Brown, Forest Grove, OR

1/2 lb. ground beef
4 3-oz. pkgs. beef-flavored
    ramen noodles,
    uncooked and divided
1 T. oil
2 eggs, beaten
1 c. pizza sauce
1/2 c. sliced black olives

25 slices pepperoni
1 c. shredded mozzarella
    cheese
1/4 c. grated Parmesan
    cheese
Optional: Italian seasoning
    to taste

Brown beef in a skillet over medium heat; drain. Remove beef from skillet and set aside. Cook noodles as directed on package; drain. Stir in 2 to 3 seasoning packets to taste, reserving the rest for another use. Add oil to skillet; heat over medium heat. Spread noodles evenly in skillet; pour eggs over noodles. Cover and cook for about 2 minutes, until eggs begin to set. Spread sauce over noodles, leaving a one-inch border around the edge. Top with beef and remaining ingredients. Cover and cook over medium-low heat until cheese is melted, about 5 to 7 minutes. Cut into wedges. Serves 4.

Salsa Chicken

Linda Shively, Hopkinsville, KY

4 boneless, skinless
  chicken breasts
1 T. plus 3/4 t. taco
  seasoning mix
1 c. mild or hot salsa
1 c. shredded Cheddar
  cheese

Garnish: sour cream
Optional: cooked Mexican
  rice, diced tomatoes,
  shredded lettuce

Place chicken breasts in a lightly greased 13"x9" baking
pan. Sprinkle taco seasoning on both sides of chicken;
pour salsa over all. Bake, uncovered, at 375 degrees for
25 to 30 minutes, until chicken is tender and juices run
clear. Sprinkle evenly with cheese; bake for an additional
5 minutes, or until cheese is melted and bubbly. Dollop
with sour cream and serve over Mexican rice and topped
with tomatoes and lettuce, if desired. Serves 4.

Sunday Meatball Skillet

Doris Stegner, Delaware, OH

3/4 lb. ground beef
1 c. onion, grated
1/2 c. Italian-flavored dry
  bread crumbs
1 egg, beaten
1/4 c. catsup
1/4 t. pepper

2 c. beef broth
1/4 c. all-purpose flour
1/2 c. sour cream
8-oz. pkg. medium egg
  noodles, cooked
Garnish: chopped fresh
  parsley

In a bowl, combine beef, onion, bread crumbs, egg,
catsup and pepper. Shape into one-inch meatballs. Spray
a skillet with non-stick vegetable spray. Cook meatballs
over medium heat, turning occasionally, until browned,
about 10 minutes. Remove meatballs and let drain on
paper towels. In a bowl, whisk together broth and flour;
add to skillet. Cook and stir until mixture thickens,
about 5 minutes. Stir in sour cream. Add meatballs and
noodles; toss to coat. Cook and stir until heated through,
about 5 minutes. Garnish with parsley. Serves 4.

Family Brats & Kraut

Angie Venable, Ostrander, OH

2 16-oz. pkgs. smoked
  bratwurst
32-oz. pkg. sauerkraut

1-1/2 c. water
pepper to taste

Combine all ingredients in a slow cooker. Cover and cook
on low setting for 3 hours. Serves 6 to 8.

Quick side

It's easy to make homemade salsa.
Pour a 15-ounce can of stewed tomatoes,
several slices of canned jalapeños and a
teaspoon or two of the jalapeño juice into
a blender. Cover and process to the desired
consistency.

Sunday Meatball Skillet

Kickin' Cajun Tilapia

Seaside Salmon Buns

Sharon Velenosi, Garden Grove, CA

14-oz. can salmon, drained
  and flaked
1/4 c. green pepper,
  chopped
1 T. onion, chopped
2 t. lemon juice

1-1/4 c. mayonnaise,
  divided
6 hamburger buns, split
12 thick tomato slices
1/2 c. shredded Cheddar
  cheese

Mix salmon, pepper, onion, lemon juice and 1/2 cup mayonnaise. Pile salmon mixture onto bun halves; top each with a tomato slice. Arrange buns on an ungreased baking sheet. Mix remaining mayonnaise with cheese; spread over tomato slices. Broil until lightly golden and cheese is melted. Serves 6.

BLT Tuna Sandwiches

Crystal Wright, Hammond, IN

7-oz. pkg. white tuna,
  drained
3 T. bacon bits
1/4 head lettuce, shredded
1 tomato, diced

1/2 to 1 c. mayonnaise
salt and pepper to taste
8 slices multi-grain bread,
  toasted
Garnish: dill pickle spears

Combine tuna, bacon, lettuce and tomato with enough mayonnaise to achieve desired consistency. Add salt and pepper to taste. Pile tuna mixture high on 4 bread slices. Top with remaining bread and serve with pickle spears. Makes 4 sandwiches.

Kickin' Cajun Tilapia

Amanda Johnson, Marysville, OH

3 T. paprika
1 T. onion powder
1 t. cayenne pepper
1 t. dried thyme
1 t. dried oregano
1/2 t. celery salt

1/8 t. garlic powder
2 t. salt
2 t. pepper
4 tilapia fillets
2 T. oil
Garnish: lemon wedges

Mix seasonings in a shallow bowl or on a plate. Press both sides of tilapia fillets into seasoning mixture; let stand for 10 minutes. Heat oil in a skillet over medium heat. Cook fillets for 4 to 6 minutes, turning once, until fish flakes easily with a fork. Remove fish to a serving plate and garnish with lemon wedges. Serves 4.

Quick tip

Visit a bakery outlet store to stock up on bread and baked goods...even pita bread and tortillas. The products are often as fresh as at your neighborhood grocery store, but at much lower prices.

Cream of Broccoli Soup

Cathy Sanders, Oakland, MD

2 c. water
2 c. broccoli, chopped
2 cubes chicken bouillon
2 T. butter
1 onion, chopped

1/2 c. all-purpose flour
2 c. milk
1-1/2 c. shredded Cheddar cheese,
  divided
salt and pepper to taste

In a large saucepan over medium heat, bring water, broccoli and bouillon to a boil. Reduce heat; simmer until broccoli is tender. Set aside saucepan without draining. Melt butter in a skillet over medium heat; sauté onion until tender. Stir in flour until smooth. Gradually stir in milk and half the cheese. Cook until thickened and creamy; add to broccoli mixture in saucepan along with remaining cheese. Add salt and pepper; heat through. Makes 4 to 6 servings.

Open-Faced Lone Star Burgers

Angie Venable, Ostrander, OH

1/4 c. onion, chopped
2 cloves garlic, minced
1/4 t. dried thyme
1-1/2 c. shredded Colby Jack
  cheese, divided

1-1/2 lbs. ground beef
6 slices frozen garlic Texas toast
8-oz. can tomato sauce
1 T. brown sugar, packed

1 t. Worcestershire sauce
1 t. steak sauce

In a large bowl, combine onion, garlic, thyme and one cup cheese. Crumble beef over top and mix well. Form into 6 oval-shaped patties. In a large skillet, cook patties over medium heat for 5 to 6 minutes per side, to desired doneness. Meanwhile, prepare toast according to package directions. Drain patties; set aside and keep warm. Add remaining ingredients to the skillet. Bring to a boil; cook and stir for 2 minutes, or until slightly thickened. Return burgers to skillet; turn to coat. Sprinkle with remaining cheese. Serve burgers on toast. Makes 6 servings.

Open-Faced Lone Star Burgers

French Onion Biscuits

French Onion Biscuits

Lane Ann Miller, Trenton, KY.

8-oz. container French
  onion dip
1/4 c. milk

1 t. dried parsley
2 c. biscuit baking mix
1 T. butter, melted

In a large bowl, whisk together onion dip, milk and
parsley until smooth. Stir in baking mix until well
blended. Drop dough by spoonfuls onto a lightly greased
baking sheet, making 12 biscuits. Bake at 450 degrees for
7 to 8 minutes, until lightly golden. Immediately brush
tops of biscuits with melted butter. Makes one dozen.

Beef Barley Soup

Sandra Antony, Washington, VA

1 lb. ground beef
1 onion, chopped
Optional: 1/2 green pepper,
  chopped
1 T. oil
6 c. water
28-oz. can crushed
  tomatoes
2 potatoes, peeled and
  diced

4 carrots, peeled and diced
1/2 c. pearled barley,
  uncooked
1 stalk celery, diced
1/2 t. dried parsley
1/2 t. dried oregano
1/2 t. dried basil
1/2 t. salt
1/2 t. pepper

In a soup pot over medium heat, brown beef, onion and
green pepper, if using, in oil. Add remaining ingredients.
Cover and simmer over low heat for 2 hours, stirring
often. Makes 8 to 10 servings.

A-to-Z Soup

Nancy Girard, Chesapeake, VA

1 onion, coarsely chopped
2 cloves garlic, minced
2 T. olive oil
1 to 2 T. Italian seasoning
4 c. beef broth
2 c. water
15-oz. can stewed tomatoes

16-oz. pkg. frozen mixed
  vegetables
1/2 c. alphabet pasta,
  uncooked
salt and pepper to taste
3 T. fresh parsley, minced

In a large soup pot over medium heat, cook onion and
garlic in oil until onion is golden, about 8 minutes. Add
seasoning to taste; cook and stir for one minute. Add
broth, water and tomatoes with juice, breaking tomatoes
up as you add them to the pot. Bring to a boil. Reduce
heat and simmer for 10 minutes. Stir in mixed vegetables
and pasta. Cover and simmer until tender, about 10 to
12 minutes. Add salt and pepper to taste; stir in parsley.
Serves 6 to 8.

Quick tip

Why not serve soup once a week...just add a
basket of warm bread for a satisfying, thrifty
dinner that everyone is sure to enjoy.

Egg & Bacon Quesadillas

Joshua Logan, Corpus Christi, TX

2 T. butter, divided
4 8-inch flour tortillas
5 eggs, beaten

1/2 c. milk
2 8-oz. pkgs. shredded
   Cheddar cheese

6 to 8 slices bacon, crisply cooked
   and crumbled
Optional: salsa, sour cream

Lightly spread about 1/4 teaspoon butter on one side of each tortilla; set aside. In a bowl, beat eggs and milk until combined. Pour egg mixture into a hot, lightly greased skillet; cook and stir over medium heat until done. Remove scrambled eggs to a dish and keep warm. Melt remaining butter in the skillet and add a tortilla, buttered-side down. Layer with 1/4 of the cheese, 1/2 of the eggs and 1/2 of the bacon. Top with 1/4 of the cheese and a tortilla, buttered-side up. Cook one to 2 minutes on each side, until golden. Repeat with remaining ingredients. Cut each into 4 wedges and serve with salsa and sour cream, if desired. Serves 4.

Egg Drop Ramen

Laura Seban, Saint Simons Island, GA

1-1/2 c. water
3-oz. pkg. chicken-flavored ramen
   noodles, uncooked and divided

2 eggs, beaten
2 slices American cheese, chopped
1/3 c. peas

In a saucepan, bring water to a boil over medium heat. Add half of the seasoning packet, reserving the rest for another use. Stir in noodles; cook for 3 minutes. Add eggs, stirring quickly for 2 minutes to break them up. Add cheese and stir in well. Remove from heat; mix in peas. Serve in soup bowls. Makes 2 to 3 servings.

Poor Man's Cordon Bleu

Linda Lamb, Round Rock, TX

8-oz. pkg. cream cheese, softened
4 green onions, minced
garlic powder to taste

6 boneless, skinless chicken
   breasts

12 slices bacon

Combine cream cheese, onions and garlic powder together; set aside. Flatten chicken breasts using a rolling pin. Spread cream cheese mixture down the enter of each chicken breast; fold chicken in half. Wrap 2 bacon slices around each chicken breast; secure with toothpicks. Arrange in an ungreased 13"x9" baking pan; bake at 350 degrees for one hour. Makes 6 servings.

Egg & Bacon Quesadillas

🥄🍴🔪 *Quick tip*
Start dinner with a cup of hot soup to take the edge off appetites...it's a super meal stretcher!

Italian Mini Meatloaves

Italian Mini Meatloaves

Cari Simons, Lawrence, KS

1 lb. ground beef
16-oz. pkg. stuffing mix
1 c. water
1 t. Italian seasoning
1 c. tomato-basil pasta
    sauce
3/4 c. shredded mozzarella
    cheese

Mix beef, stuffing mix, water and seasoning together until well blended. Spray a muffin tin with non-stick vegetable spray. Press mixture evenly into 12 muffin cups. Make a small well in the center of each; spoon some sauce into each well. Bake, uncovered, at 375 degrees for about 30 minutes, until cooked through. Sprinkle with cheese and bake for 5 to 7 more minutes, until cheese is melted. Makes 6 servings.

German Potato Pancakes

Elaine Nichols, Mesa, AZ

4 potatoes, peeled and
    coarsely grated
1/4 c. milk
1 egg, beaten
1 onion, diced
2 T. all-purpose flour
salt and pepper to taste
oil for frying

Combine all ingredients except oil; mix well with a fork and set aside. Heat 1/4 inch oil in a deep skillet over medium-high heat. For each pancake, spread about 2 heaping tablespoonfuls into a circle in skillet. Cook for 3 to 4 minutes, until golden; turn and cook on other side. Drain on paper towels. Serves 4 to 6.

Cheese-Filled Ravioli

Lisa Bakos, Stephens City, VA

1 lb. ricotta cheese
6 eggs, divided
fresh parsley, minced, to
    taste
1/2 to 3/4 c. grated Romano
    cheese
salt and pepper to taste
3 c. all-purpose flour
1 T. water
Garnish: warm marinara
    sauce, grated Romano
    cheese

Mix ricotta, one egg, parsley, Romano cheese, salt and pepper; set aside. Place flour in a large bowl; make a well in the center. Fill well with remaining eggs; blend mixture with a fork. When eggs are thoroughly mixed, add water as needed to make a dough. Divide dough into 2 balls. Roll out onto a floured surface and cut into squares with a knife or pizza cutter. Fill each with one tablespoon cheese mixture; fold over and press ends together with a floured fork. Cook in boiling water for 15 minutes; drain. Serve with warm marinara sauce and grated Romano cheese. Serves 6.

Stuffed Chicken Breasts

Ursala Armstrong, Odenville, AL

4 boneless, skinless chicken
  breasts

8-oz. container garlic & herb
  cream cheese spread

8 slices bacon

Flatten chicken breasts between wax paper. Spread each chicken breast with cream cheese and roll up. Wrap 2 slices bacon around each roll; secure with toothpicks. Place on a grill or in a grill pan over medium heat. Cook, turning occasionally, until golden and chicken juices run clear, about 20 to 25 minutes. Serves 4.

Loaded Mashed Potato Casserole

Nancy Girard, Chesapeake, VA

5 to 6 potatoes, peeled and cubed
1/2 c. milk
8-oz. pkg. cream cheese, softened
8-oz. container sour cream

2 t. dried parsley
1 t. garlic salt
1/4 t. nutmeg
3/4 c. shredded Cheddar cheese

12 slices bacon, crisply cooked and
  crumbled

Cover potatoes with water in a large saucepan; bring to boil over medium heat. Reduce heat; simmer for 20 to 25 minutes. Drain well. Mash until light and fluffy. In a large bowl, beat together all ingredients except Cheddar cheese and bacon until smooth and creamy. Spoon into a lightly greased 13"x9" baking pan; sprinkle with cheese and bacon. Cover and bake at 350 degrees for 30 minutes, or until heated through. Serves 10 to 12.

Loaded Mashed Potato Casserole

Quick tip

For healthy, filling side dishes, try whole grains like barley and brown rice. They're high in protein and, with the addition of different seasonings, adapt readily to many tasty flavors.

Tomato & Chicken Penne

Quick tip

Canned tomatoes are economical, delicious and are even available already seasoned...that's like getting herbs and spices free! They're often a better choice than less-than-ripe fresh tomatoes.

Tomato & Chicken Penne

Stefani St. Pierre, South Dennis, MA

1/4 c. olive oil
1 t. garlic, chopped
28-oz. can diced tomatoes, drained
1/2 c. fresh basil, chopped

2 lbs. boneless, skinless chicken breasts, cooked and cubed
16-oz. pkg. penne pasta, cooked

8-oz. pkg. shredded mozzarella cheese
salt and pepper to taste

Heat oil in a skillet over medium heat. Add garlic; sauté for one minute. Stir in tomatoes and basil; continue cooking for 2 minutes. Add chicken to skillet. Sauté for about 5 minutes, until heated through. Transfer chicken mixture to a large serving bowl; toss with pasta and cheese. Season with salt and pepper. Makes 6 to 8 servings.

Chicken Taco Salad

Abby Snay, San Francisco, CA

8 6-inch flour tortillas
2 c. cooked chicken breast, shredded
1-1/4 oz. pkg. taco seasoning mix
3/4 c. water
2 c. shredded lettuce

15-1/2 oz. can black beans, drained and rinsed
1-1/2 c. shredded Cheddar cheese
2 tomatoes, chopped
1/2 c. green onion, sliced
15-1/4 oz. can corn, drained

2-1/4 oz. can sliced black olives, drained
1 avocado, pitted, peeled and cubed
Garnish: sour cream, salsa

Microwave tortillas on high setting for one minute, or until softened. Press each tortilla into an ungreased jumbo muffin cup to form a bowl shape. Bake at 350 degrees for 10 minutes; cool. Combine chicken, taco seasoning and water in a skillet over medium heat. Cook, stirring frequently, until blended, about 5 minutes. Divide lettuce among tortilla bowls. Top with chicken and other ingredients, garnishing with a dollop of sour cream and salsa. Makes 8 servings.

Tortellini Spinach Soup

Lois Valeri, Sicklerville, NJ

2 cloves garlic, minced
1 T. olive oil
2 14-1/2 oz. cans chicken broth
14-1/2 oz. can stewed tomatoes
9-oz. pkg. cheese tortellini, uncooked
10-oz. pkg. frozen chopped spinach, thawed and drained
salt and pepper to taste

In a large soup pot over medium-high heat, sauté garlic in oil for 2 to 3 minutes. Add broth and tomatoes with juice; turn heat up to high and bring to a boil. Stir in tortellini and cook according to package instructions. When tortellini is almost done, add spinach; heat through. Add salt and pepper to taste. Makes 6 servings.

Stuffed Cabbage Soup

Carolyn Helewski, Arcadia, FL

1 lb. ground beef
garlic powder, salt and pepper to taste
2 14-1/2 oz. cans beef broth
3-2/3 c. water
2 10-3/4 oz. cans tomato soup
14.4-oz. can sauerkraut
1/2 head cabbage, chopped
1 c. cooked rice

Brown beef in a large soup pot over medium heat; drain. Sprinkle with garlic powder, salt and pepper. Add broth, water, soup and undrained sauerkraut; stir until mixed well. Mix in cabbage and cooked rice; bring to a boil. Lower heat and simmer for one hour. Makes 10 servings.

Fluffy Whole-Wheat Biscuits

Mary Gage, Wakewood, CA

1 c. all-purpose flour
1 c. whole-wheat flour
4 t. baking powder
1 T. sugar
3/4 t. salt
1/4 c. butter
1 c. milk

Combine flours, baking powder, sugar and salt; mix well. Cut in butter until mixture resembles coarse crumbs. Stir in milk just until moistened. Turn dough out onto a lightly floured surface; knead gently 8 to 10 times. Roll out to 3/4-inch thickness. Cut with a 2-1/2" round biscuit cutter. Place biscuits on an ungreased baking sheet. Bake at 450 degrees for 10 to 12 minutes, until lightly golden. Serve warm. Makes one dozen.

Tortellini Spinach Soup

Hot Chicken Sandwiches

Hot Chicken Sandwiches

Kelly Patrick, Gallipolis, OH

6-oz. pkg. chicken-flavored
  stuffing mix
6-oz. pkg. herb-flavored
  stuffing mix
12-1/2 oz. can chicken,
  drained and flaked
10-3/4 oz. can cream
  of chicken soup
8 to 10 sandwich
  buns, split

In a stockpot, prepare stuffing mixes as packages direct. Mix in chicken and soup. Increase heat to medium; cook and stir until heated through. Serve on buns. Serves 8 to 10.

Roasted Chicken & Apples

Cathy Hillier, Salt Lake City, UT

5 c. apples, peeled, cored
  and chopped
1 t. fresh sage, chopped
1/4 t. cinnamon
1/8 t. nutmeg
4 cloves garlic, chopped
1/2 t. salt, divided
8 skinless chicken thighs
1/4 t. pepper

In a large bowl, combine apples, seasonings and garlic with 1/4 teaspoon salt; toss well to coat. Spread on a 15"x10" jelly-roll pan sprayed with non-stick vegetable spray. Season chicken with remaining salt and pepper; arrange on top of apple mixture. Bake, uncovered, at 475 degrees for 25 minutes, or until juices run clear when chicken is pierced with a fork. Makes 8 servings.

Chicken Turnovers

Angela Bettencourt, Mukilteo, WA

4 c. cooked chicken, cubed
8-oz. pkg. cream cheese,
  softened
1/2 c. milk
1 T. onion, minced
1 t. salt
1/8 t. pepper
2 8-oz. tubes refrigerated
  crescent rolls
1 T. margarine, melted
3/4 c. grated Parmesan
  cheese
2 10-3/4 oz. cans cream
  of chicken soup
2/3 c. milk

Blend chicken, cream cheese, milk, onion, salt and pepper; set aside. Separate each tube of crescent rolls into 4 rectangles; press to seal perforations. Spoon 1/2 cup chicken mixture into center of each rectangle; pull up corners to form a triangle and press to seal. Place turnovers on an ungreased baking sheet. Brush tops with margarine; sprinkle with Parmesan. Bake, uncovered, at 350 degrees for 20 to 25 minutes, until golden. While turnovers are baking, combine soup and milk in a saucepan; heat until bubbly. Spoon soup mixture over turnovers. Serves 4 to 6.

Quick tip

If you often use chopped onion, celery and green pepper to add flavor to sautéed dishes, save time by chopping lots at once. Create your own sauté blend and freeze it in a plastic freezer container. Add it to skillet dishes straight from the freezer...there's no need to thaw.

Vickie's Enchilada Bake

Vickie

15-oz. can chili with beans

2 10-oz. cans enchilada sauce

2 T. onion, grated

12-oz. pkg. nacho cheese tortilla chips, crushed and divided

2-1/2 c. shredded Cheddar cheese, divided

1-1/4 c. sour cream

Combine chili, enchilada sauce and onion in a large bowl. Set aside 2 cups crushed chips and 1/2 cup cheese for topping; add remaining chips and cheese to chili mixture. Spoon mixture into a greased 11"x9" baking pan. Bake, uncovered, at 375 degrees for 20 minutes, until hot and bubbly. Remove from oven; top with sour cream, remaining chips and remaining cheese. Return to oven until cheese is melted. Serves 6.

Mexican Braid

Kristin Stone, Davis, CA

1 lb. ground turkey

10-oz. can diced tomatoes with green chiles, drained

1 onion, chopped

1 c. corn

2 loaves frozen bread dough, thawed

8-oz. pkg. shredded Pepper Jack cheese

Brown turkey with tomatoes and onion in a skillet over medium heat; drain. Add corn; cook until heated through. Roll out each loaf of dough to 1/4-inch thickness. Transfer to baking sheets that have been lined with lightly greased aluminum foil. Cut diagonal slits along each side of the dough, about one inch apart and 3 inches deep. Place half of turkey mixture in the center of each piece of dough. Top each with half of cheese. Fold in short sides of dough, pinching to seal. Fold dough flaps over the turkey mixture, alternating sides and creating a braided pattern. Pinch edges to seal. Bake at 350 degrees for 25 to 30 minutes, until golden. Serves 16.

Crowd-Size Pizza Hot Dish

Beth Bundy, Long Prairie, MN

6 c. elbow macaroni, uncooked

3 lbs. ground beef

1 onion, chopped

3 15-oz. cans tomato sauce

1-1/2 T. salt

1 T. pepper

1 T. dried oregano

2 t. garlic powder

3 eggs, beaten

1-1/2 c. milk

2 16-oz. pkgs. shredded Cheddar cheese

Cook macaroni according to package directions; drain. Place in a large bowl and set aside. In a skillet over medium heat, brown beef and onion together; drain. Stir in tomato sauce and seasonings; blend well. Simmer for 5 to 10 minutes, stirring occasionally. Whisk eggs and milk together; blend into macaroni. Add beef mixture and stir well. Transfer into 2 greased 13"x9" baking pans. Top with cheese. Bake, uncovered, at 350 degrees for 20 minutes, or until heated through. Let stand 10 minutes before cutting. Makes 30 servings.

Quick tip

Spicy barbecue potato chips make a tasty topping for Mexican casseroles...just crush 'em up and sprinkle on.

Mexican Braid

Skillet Chicken-Fried Rice

Baked Quesadillas

Patti Walker, Mocksville, NC

2 8-oz. cans chicken, drained
  and flaked
1 to 2 T. taco seasoning mix

8-oz. jar salsa
8-oz. pkg. shredded Mexican-blend
  cheese

16 8-inch flour tortillas
Garnish: sour cream, avocado
  slices

Mix chicken, taco seasoning, salsa and cheese. Arrange 8 tortillas on baking sheets sprayed with non-stick vegetable spray. Spread chicken mixture onto tortillas. Top with remaining tortillas. Spray tops with non-stick vegetable spray. Bake at 350 degrees for 5 to 10 minutes, until tops are golden. Allow to cool for a few minutes; cut into quarters. Garnish with sour cream and avocado slices. Makes 8 servings.

Skillet Chicken-Fried Rice

Nicole Sampson, Tiskilwa, IL

1 T. oil
2 eggs, beaten
1/2 c. frozen peas
1/2 c. carrot, peeled and sliced

1/4 c. onion, diced
2 c. cooked rice
1 c. cooked chicken, cubed
2 T. soy sauce

1 T. stir-fry sauce
1/4 t. garlic, minced

Heat oil in a large skillet over medium heat. Scramble eggs in oil. When eggs are set, remove from pan and chop. Lightly spray the same skillet with non-stick cooking spray and place over medium heat. Add peas, carrot and onion to skillet. Cook for 2 to 3 minutes, until vegetables are crisp-tender. Add chopped scrambled eggs and remaining ingredients to vegetable mixture. Cook, stirring occasionally, until mixture is heated through. Makes 4 servings.

Easy Tamale Casserole

Jan Durston, Norco, CA

12 frozen tamales, partially
  thawed

2 14-3/4 oz. cans creamed corn
8-oz. can chiles

2 c. shredded Cheddar cheese

Slice tamales in half lengthwise; arrange half with the cut-side up in an ungreased 13"x9" baking pan. Spread one can creamed corn and chiles on top; layer on remaining tamale halves, cut-side down. Spread with remaining can creamed corn; bake at 350 degrees until bubbly, about 30 to 40 minutes. Sprinkle with cheese; return to oven until melted, about 5 to 8 minutes. Serves 6.

Dagwood Burgers

Jennifer Scott, Checotah, OK

2 lbs. lean ground beef
1 lb. Italian ground pork
 sausage
2 c. dry bread crumbs
1 onion, chopped
1/2 c. barbecue sauce
1 egg, beaten

1.35-oz. pkg. onion soup
 mix
1 t. jalapeño pepper, diced
salt and pepper to taste
12 to 15 hamburger buns,
 split

Mix all ingredients except salt, pepper and buns in a very
large bowl. Form into 12 to 15 patties; sprinkle with salt
and pepper. Place on a charcoal grill or in a skillet over
medium heat. Cook burgers to desired doneness. Serve
on buns. Makes 12 to 15 sandwiches.

Goalpost Apple Slaw

Mary Romack, Ann Arbor, MI

2-1/4 c. red apples, cored
 and cubed
2-1/4 c. green apples, cored
 and cubed
1 c. coleslaw mix
1/3 c. sweetened dried
 cranberries
1/3 c. chopped walnuts

1 c. sour cream
3 T. lemon juice
1 to 2 T. vinegar
1 T. sugar
1 T. poppy seed
3/4 t. salt
1/8 t. pepper

Lightly toss ingredients in a large bowl until well mixed.
Chill for at least one hour before serving. Serves 6 to 8.

Hamburger Crunch

Gayle Ortmeyer, Jefferson City, MO

2 lbs. ground beef
1 T. onion, minced
2 10-3/4 oz. cans tomato
 soup

1 t. chili powder
4 c. corn chips
8-oz. pkg. shredded
 Cheddar cheese

Brown ground beef and onion together in a large skillet
over medium heat; drain. Stir in soup and chili powder.
Spread in an ungreased 13"x9" baking pan; top with
corn chips. Bake, uncovered, at 350 degrees for 20 to
25 minutes. Remove from oven; sprinkle with cheese.
Bake for an additional 5 minutes, until cheese melts.
Serves 6 to 8.

Quick tip

Foods at a dinner party don't have to be
fancy...your guests will be delighted with
comfort foods like Grandma used to make!

Goalpost Apple Slaw

Corn Surprise

🥄🍴🔪 *Quick tip*

When there's extra cooked macaroni or pasta left over, it's fine to freeze it for later. Drain well, toss with a little oil and freeze in a plastic zipping bag. To use, place the frozen pasta in a colander, rinse it with hot water to separate and stir into a skillet dish or casserole.

Twistin' Tuna Bake

Marilyn Morel, Keene, NH

1 c. Alfredo sauce
2 eggs, beaten
1 t. garlic powder
8-oz. pkg. rotini pasta, cooked

10-oz. pkg. frozen chopped
  broccoli, thawed and drained
6-oz. can tuna, drained and flaked

1 c. round buttery crackers,
  crushed
3 T. butter, melted

Combine sauce, eggs and garlic powder; blend thoroughly. Add pasta, broccoli and tuna; turn into a lightly greased 8"x8" baking pan. Toss together cracker crumbs and butter; sprinkle over top of casserole. Bake, uncovered, at 350 degrees for 20 minutes, or until bubbly and heated through. Serves 6.

Corn Surprise

Eva Rae Walters, Paola, KS

15-1/4 oz. can corn
8-oz. pkg. small pasta shells,
  uncooked

16-oz. can cream-style corn
8-oz. pkg. shredded
  Mexican-blend cheese

Combine undrained corn and remaining ingredients in a bowl. Transfer to a greased 13"x9" baking pan. Bake, covered, at 350 degrees for 45 minutes, or until pasta is tender. As it bakes, stir casserole several times; uncover for the last 10 minutes of cooking. Serves 6 to 8.

Cobb Salad Subs

Jo Ann

1-1/3 c. cooked chicken, diced
2 roma tomatoes, diced
4 slices bacon, crisply cooked and crumbled
1/2 c. crumbled blue cheese
2 eggs, hard-boiled, peeled and diced
4 submarine buns, split and toasted
4 leaves lettuce

Combine all ingredients except buns and lettuce. Drizzle with Avocado Dressing and toss to coat. Spoon mixture over bottom halves of buns; add lettuce leaves and top halves of buns. Makes 4 sandwiches.

Avocado Dressing:
3 T. olive oil
1 T. white wine vinegar
1 t. Dijon mustard
1/2 t. salt
1/2 t. pepper
1 avocado, pitted, peeled and diced

In a bowl, combine all ingredients except avocado; whisk until well blended. Stir in avocado.

Simple Scalloped Tomatoes

Joan White, Malvern, PA

1 onion, chopped
1/4 c. butter
28-oz. can diced tomatoes
5 slices bread, lightly toasted and cubed
1/4 c. brown sugar, packed
1/2 t. salt
1/4 t. pepper

Cook onion in butter until just tender, but not browned. Combine onion mixture with tomatoes and their juice in a bowl; add remaining ingredients and mix well. Pour into a greased 8"x8" baking pan. Bake, uncovered, at 350 degrees for 45 minutes. Makes 4 to 6 servings.

Chicken Presto

Kathy Grashoff, Fort Wayne, IN

2 T. oil
3 c. sliced mushrooms
1 onion, chopped
15-oz. can stewed tomatoes
1/4 c. Italian salad dressing
3 T. tomato paste
4 boneless, skinless chicken breasts
1 c. shredded mozzarella cheese
2 slices bacon, crisply cooked and crumbled

Heat oil in a large skillet over medium-high heat. Add mushrooms and onion; cook for 5 minutes, stirring occasionally. Stir in tomatoes with juice, salad dressing and tomato paste. Add chicken and cover; reduce heat to medium-low. Simmer for about 12 minutes, until chicken is cooked through. Sprinkle with cheese and bacon; simmer, uncovered, for 5 minutes longer. Serves 4.

Cobb Salad Subs

Baked Spinach & Rice

🥄🍴🔪 *Quick side*

A simple vinaigrette dressing adds zest to tossed green salads and veggies. It's easy to make too. Combine 2 tablespoons cider vinegar and 6 tablespoons olive oil in a small jar, twist on the lid and shake well. Add salt and pepper to taste...even stir in a teaspoon of Dijon mustard or minced fresh basil.

Louisiana Red Beans & Rice

Diana Chaney, Olathe, KS

2 15-oz. cans red beans
14-1/2 oz. can diced tomatoes
1/2 c. celery, chopped
1/2 c. green pepper, chopped

1/2 c. green onion, chopped
2 cloves garlic, minced
1 to 2 t. hot pepper sauce
1 t. Worcestershire sauce

1 bay leaf
cooked rice

Combine all ingredients except rice in a slow cooker; do not drain beans and tomatoes. Cover and cook on low setting for 4 to 6 hours. About 30 minutes before serving, use a potato masher to mash mixture slightly until thickened. Cover again; increase heat to high setting and continue cooking for 30 minutes. Discard bay leaf. To serve, ladle over cooked rice in bowls. Makes 6 servings.

Baked Spinach & Rice

Elena Smith, Monterey, CA

10-oz. pkg. frozen chopped
  spinach, thawed and well
  drained
2 c. cooked rice

8-oz. pkg. pasteurized process
  cheese spread, cubed
1/3 c. onion, chopped
1/3 c. red pepper, chopped

3 eggs, beaten
1/8 t. pepper
Optional: 1/4 lb. turkey bacon,
  crisply cooked and crumbled

In a large bowl, combine all ingredients, mixing well. Spread in a greased 10"x6" baking pan; smooth top with a spatula. Bake, uncovered, at 350 degrees for 30 minutes. Let stand 5 minutes; cut into squares. Makes 8 servings.

Divine Praline Brownies

Sandy Bernards, Valencia, CA

22-1/2 oz. pkg. brownie mix
1/4 c. butter

1 c. brown sugar, packed

1 c. chopped pecans

Prepare brownie mix according to package directions. Spread batter in a greased 13"x9" baking pan. Set aside. Melt butter in a skillet over low heat; add brown sugar and pecans. Heat until sugar dissolves; drizzle over brownie batter. Bake at 350 degrees for 25 to 30 minutes. Cool and cut into bars. Keep refrigerated. Makes 12 to 15.

Minty Chocolate Brownies

Kristy Markners, Fort Mill, SC

1/2 c. butter, melted
1 c. sugar
1 t. vanilla extract
2 eggs

1/2 c. all-purpose flour
1/3 c. baking cocoa
1/4 t. baking powder
1/4 t. salt

1/4 c. milk
7 chocolate-covered thin mint
  cookies, crushed

In a bowl, beat together butter, sugar and vanilla with an electric mixer on medium speed. Beat in eggs, one at a time, until fully combined. In a separate bowl, stir together flour, cocoa, baking powder and salt. Slowly add flour mixture to butter mixture, beating until well blended. Beat in milk. Fold in crushed cookies. Spread batter evenly in a lightly greased 9"x9" baking pan. Bake at 350 degrees for 35 to 40 minutes, until a toothpick inserted near the center tests clean. Cool completely in pan on a wire rack. Cut into squares. Makes one dozen.

Quick tip

When you find butter and nuts on sale, tuck extras into the freezer. They'll stay fresh-tasting for months.

Divine Praline Brownies

Orange Puff Cupcakes

Orange Puff Cupcakes

Heather Roberts, Quebec, Canada

1/3 c. margarine
1 c. sugar
2 eggs, beaten
1-3/4 c. all-purpose flour
1 T. baking powder
1/2 c. frozen orange juice concentrate, thawed
Optional: zest of 1 orange
Garnish: white frosting, orange zest strips

Beat together margarine and sugar in a bowl; add eggs. Combine flour and baking powder; add alternately with orange juice to margarine mixture. Stir in zest, if using. Fill paper-lined muffin cups 2/3 full. Bake at 375 degrees for 15 minutes. Let cool. Spread with frosting and garnish with orange zest strips, if desired. Makes one dozen.

Hannah's Oatmeal Cookies

Katie Majeske, Denver, PA

1 c. butter, softened
1 c. sugar
1 c. brown sugar, packed
2 eggs
1 t. almond or caramel pecan extract
2 c. all-purpose flour
1 t. baking soda
1 t. salt
1-1/2 t. cinnamon
3 c. quick-cooking oats, uncooked
1-1/2 c. chocolate-covered raisins

Blend together butter and sugars. Beat in eggs, one at a time; stir in extract. In a separate bowl, combine flour, baking soda, salt and cinnamon; stir flour mixture into butter mixture. Mix in oats; fold in raisins. Form dough into walnut-size balls; place 2 inches apart on ungreased baking sheets. Bake at 375 degrees for 8 to 10 minutes. Allow cookies to cool on baking sheets for 5 minutes; transfer to a wire rack to cool completely. Makes 2 to 3 dozen.

Frosted Sugar Cookies

June Lemen, Nashua, NH

2 c. butter, softened
1-1/3 c. sugar
2 eggs, beaten
2 t. vanilla extract
5 c. all-purpose flour
Garnish: colored sugar

Blend butter and sugar together; stir in eggs and vanilla. Add flour; mix until well blended. Shape into a ball; cover and chill for 4 hours to overnight. Roll out dough 1/4-inch thick on a lightly floured surface; cut out with cookie cutters as desired. Arrange cookies on lightly greased baking sheets. Bake at 350 degrees for 8 to 10 minutes, until golden. Frost cookies when cool; decorate as desired. Makes 4 dozen.

Frosting:
4-1/2 c. powdered sugar
6 T. butter, melted
6 T. milk
2 T. vanilla extract
1 T. lemon juice
Optional: food coloring

Combine all ingredients in a medium bowl. Beat with an electric mixer on low speed until smooth.

Simple Sweets

Summertime Strawberry Shortcake

Martha Doyle, Rome, NY

3 to 4 c. strawberries,
  hulled and sliced

1/2 c. plus 2 T. sugar,
  divided

2 c. all-purpose flour

1 T. baking powder

1/2 t. salt

3/4 c. butter, divided

1 egg, beaten

2/3 c. light cream

1 c. whipping cream,
  whipped

Toss strawberries with 1/2 cup sugar and set aside.
Combine flour, remaining sugar, baking powder and salt
in a separate bowl. Cut in 1/2 cup butter until mixture
forms coarse crumbs; set aside. Whisk together egg
and light cream; add to flour mixture, stirring just until
moistened. Divide dough into 6 parts; pat into biscuits
and place on a greased baking sheet. Bake at 450 degrees
for 8 to 10 minutes, until golden. Cool biscuits briefly on
a wire rack. Split in half with a serrated knife; spread
bottoms with remaining butter. Top with berries and
whipped cream; add tops. Garnish with remaining
berries and cream. Makes 6 servings.

Berry Peachy Twists

Cyndy Wilber, Ravena, NY

8-oz. tube refrigerated
  crescent rolls

2 T. butter, melted

3-oz. pkg. strawberry
  gelatin mix

15-oz. can sliced peaches,
  drained and cubed

Separate rolls into 8 triangles. Brush triangles with
melted butter; sprinkle with gelatin mix and top evenly
with peaches. Roll up each triangle into a crescent as
directed on package. Arrange on a large greased baking
sheet. Bake at 350 degrees for 12 to 15 minutes, until
golden. Let cool slightly before serving. Makes
8 servings.

Blueberry Pound Cake

Suzy Grubich, Eighty Four, PA

2-1/2 c. sugar

1/2 c. butter, softened

2 t. vanilla

8-oz. pkg. cream cheese,
  softened

4 eggs

2 c. fresh blueberries

3 c. all-purpose flour,
  divided

1 t. baking powder

1/2 t. baking soda

1/2 t. salt

8-oz. container lemon
  yogurt

Beat sugar, butter, vanilla and cream cheese with an
electric mixer on medium speed until blended. Beat in
eggs one at a time. Toss blueberries with 2 tablespoons
flour; set aside. Combine remaining flour, baking
powder, baking soda and salt. Add flour mixtures
to sugar mixture alternately with yogurt. Fold in
blueberries; pour into greased tube pan. Bake at
350 degrees for one hour, or until a toothpick tests clean.
Cool cake in pan for 10 minutes; turn out. Drizzle with
icing while still warm. Serves 16.

Icing:

1/2 c. powdered sugar

4 t. lemon juice

Prepare icing by combining ingredients to drizzling
consistency.

Quick tip

Homebaked goodies are always a welcome
gift. For a fun and frugal presentation, run
brightly colored leftover wrapping paper
through a paper shredder. Use it to fill a
gift bag and tuck in a stack of plastic-
wrapped cookies.

Blueberry Pound Cake

Marshmallow Treats on a Stick

Mini Pie Bites

Krissy Mosqueda, Houston, TX

15-oz. pkg. frozen pie
  crust, thawed and
  unbaked
1 c. favorite-flavor fruit pie
  filling
1 T. milk
1/2 c. powdered sugar

Unroll pie crusts; cut into 12 equal squares. Spoon
one to 2 teaspoons pie filling into the center of each
square. Bring the corners of each square together above
filling; pinch together corners and seams to seal. Place
each mini pie into an ungreased muffin cup. Bake at
450 degrees for 11 to 14 minutes, until golden; cool.
Meanwhile, in a bowl, slowly whisk milk into powdered
sugar until a glaze consistency is reached. Using a fork,
drizzle glaze over bites. Let stand for about 20 minutes
before serving. Makes 2 dozen.

Delectable Peanut Butter Squares

Lyn Peters, Olive Hill, KY

1/2 c. butter
1/2 c. brown sugar, packed
2 c. creamy or crunchy
  peanut butter
1 t. vanilla extract
2-1/2 c. powdered sugar
6-oz. pkg. semi-sweet
  chocolate chips

Melt butter in a large saucepan over low heat, stirring
to prevent burning. Add brown sugar; stir until
completely dissolved. Add peanut butter and vanilla;
mix thoroughly. Add powdered sugar; stir well. Press
mixture into a 13"x9" baking pan sprayed with
non-stick vegetable spray; let cool. Melt chocolate chips
in a double boiler over low heat; spread evenly over
peanut butter layer. Let cool completely; cut into squares.
Makes one to 2 dozen.

Marshmallow Treats on a Stick

Martha Stapler, Sanford, FL

14-oz. pkg. caramels,
  unwrapped
14-oz. can sweetened
  condensed milk
13-1/2 oz. pkg. crispy rice
  cereal
24 marshmallows
wooden skewers or fondue
  forks

Combine caramels and condensed milk in a saucepan
over low heat. Cook, stirring occasionally, until caramels
are melted. Remove from heat. Pour cereal into a large
bowl. Place each marshmallow on a wooden skewer or
fondue fork. Dip marshmallow in caramel; roll in cereal.
Place coated marshmallows on parchment paper to cool.
Makes 2 dozen.

Quick tip

One of the secrets of a happy life is
continuous small treats.
-Iris Murdoch

Raspberry Custard Pie

Sarah Swanson, Noblesville, IN

2 eggs, beaten
8-oz. container sour cream
1-1/2 to 2 c. fresh raspberries

1 c. sugar
1 T. all-purpose flour
1/2 t. salt

9-inch pie crust, unbaked

Whisk together eggs and sour cream in a large bowl; set aside. In a separate bowl, combine raspberries, sugar, flour and salt; toss lightly. Add berry mixture to sour cream mixture; mix well and pour into unbaked crust. Bake at 350 degrees for 45 minutes, or until firm and golden. Cool completely. Serves 6 to 8.

Very Berry Peach Pies

Wanda Niles, Costa Mesa, CA

4 c. peaches, peeled, pitted and
   sliced
1-1/2 c. blackberries

1 c. blueberries
3/4 c. plus 2 t. sugar, divided
1/4 c. all-purpose flour

2 T. butter, diced
2 9-inch pie crusts
Garnish: cinnamon-sugar

Combine fruit in a large bowl; mix gently. Blend 3/4 cup sugar and flour in a small bowl; toss lightly with fruit mixture. Pour fruit mixture into six to eight, 3" individual ramekins; dot with butter. Gently roll out dough on a floured surface and cut 6 to 8 circles one inch larger than ramekins. Place crusts atop ramekins. Trim and crimp edges; cut vents in crust. Sprinkle with cinnamon-sugar. Cover edges of crust with strips of aluminum foil to prevent over browning. Bake at 425 degrees for 40 to 45 minutes, until golden. Makes 6 to 8 servings.

Raspberry Custard Pie

Skillet Cherry Pie

Skillet Cherry Pie

Pearl Teiserskas, Brookfield, IL

1/4 c. butter
1/2 c. brown sugar, packed
2 9-inch frozen pie crusts, unbaked
15-oz. can tart cherries, drained
21-oz. can cherry pie filling

1/4 c. sugar
1 T. plus 1/8 t. all-purpose flour
1 to 2 T. milk
Garnish: powdered sugar

In a cast-iron skillet, melt butter with brown sugar over medium-low heat. Remove from heat. Place one frozen pie crust in skillet on top of butter mixture; set aside. In a bowl, mix cherries and pie filling; spoon into crust. Mix sugar and flour together in a cup; sprinkle evenly over cherry mixture. Place remaining frozen pie crust upside-down on top of cherry mixture. Brush with milk; cut slits in crust to vent. Bake at 350 degrees for one hour, or until bubbly and crust is golden. Cool; sprinkle with powdered sugar. Serves 8.

Grandma's Peach Cobbler

Wendell Mays, Barboursville, WV

1/2 c. butter, sliced
15-1/4 oz. can sliced peaches in syrup
1 c. self-rising flour
1 c. sugar

1 c. whole milk
1 t. almond extract
cinnamon to taste
Optional: whipping cream or vanilla ice cream

Add butter to an 11"x7" baking pan; melt in a 350-degree oven. Pour peaches with syrup into pan; set aside. In a bowl, combine flour, sugar, milk and extract; stir until smooth. Pour batter over peaches. Bake at 350 degrees until bubbly and golden, about 35 to 45 minutes. Remove from oven; immediately sprinkle with cinnamon. Serve warm, topped with cream or ice cream, if desired. Serves 6 to 8.

Easy Cherry Cobbler

Melanie Klosterhoff, Fairbanks, AK

15-oz. can tart red cherries
1 c. all-purpose flour
1-1/4 c. sugar, divided
1 c. milk
2 t. baking powder

1/8 t. salt
1/2 c. butter, melted
Optional: vanilla ice cream or whipped cream

In a saucepan over medium heat, cook cherries with their juice until boiling; remove from heat. In a medium bowl, mix flour, one cup sugar, milk, baking powder and salt. Spread butter in a 2-quart casserole dish or in 4 to 6 one-cup ramekins; pour flour mixture over butter. Add cherries; do not stir. Sprinkle remaining sugar over top. Bake at 400 degrees for 20 to 30 minutes. Serve warm, garnished as desired. Makes 4 to 6 servings.

Quick tip

Bake up lots of pies and cobblers...they can be frozen and enjoyed as much as 4 months later! Cool completely, then wrap in plastic wrap and two layers of aluminum foil before freezing. To serve, thaw overnight in the fridge, bring to room temperature and rewarm in the oven.

Easiest Boston Cream Cupcakes

Robin Hill, Rochester, NY

18-1/4 oz. pkg. yellow cake mix
3.4-oz. pkg. instant vanilla
   pudding mix

1 c. cold milk
1-1/2 c. frozen whipped topping,
   thawed and divided

4 1-oz. sqs. semi-sweet baking
   chocolate

Prepare cake mix according to package directions. Fill greased muffin cups 2/3 full and bake at 350 degrees for 15 to 20 minutes. Cool completely. Whisk pudding mix and milk for 2 minutes; let stand 5 minutes. Use a serrated knife to cut off the top of each cupcake; set tops aside. Stir 1/2 cup whipped topping into pudding. Spoon one tablespoon onto each cupcake; replace cupcake tops. In a microwave-safe bowl, combine remaining whipped topping and chocolate. Microwave for one minute; stir and microwave an additional 30 seconds. Stir until chocolate is melted; let stand 15 minutes. Frost cupcakes with chocolate mixture. Makes 2 dozen.

Peaches & Cream Pie

Lori Ritchey, Denver, PA

3/4 c. all-purpose flour
1 t. baking powder
1/2 t. salt
3-oz. pkg. cook & serve vanilla
   pudding mix

3 T. butter, softened
1 egg
1/2 c. milk
16-oz. can sliced peaches, drained
   and 5 T. juice reserved

8-oz. pkg. cream cheese, softened
1/2 c. sugar
Garnish: cinnamon-sugar to taste

Combine flour, baking powder, salt, dry pudding mix, butter, egg and milk in a large bowl; beat with an electric mixer for 2 minutes. Pour into a greased 9" pie plate. Arrange peach slices on top; set aside. Beat together cream cheese, sugar and reserved juice for 2 minutes. Spoon over peaches; sprinkle with cinnamon-sugar. Bake at 350 degrees for 30 minutes. Serves 8.

🥄🍴🔪

Quick tip

Vanilla extract is a must in all kinds of baked treats! Save by purchasing a large bottle of vanilla at a club store. Ounce for ounce, it's much cheaper than buying the tiny bottles sold in the supermarket baking aisle.

Easiest Boston Cream Cupcakes

German Chocolate Delights

Salted Peanut Cookies
Marilyn Barnes, Upper Sandusky, OH

1 c. brown sugar, packed
1 c. sugar
1 c. butter, softened
2 eggs, beaten
1 t. vanilla extract
2 c. all-purpose flour
1 t. baking powder
1 t. baking soda
1 c. corn flake cereal, crushed
1 c. long-cooking oats, uncooked
1 c. salted peanuts

Blend together sugars and butter in a large bowl. Add eggs and vanilla; set aside. In a separate bowl, sift together flour, baking powder and baking soda. Add flour mixture to sugar mixture and stir well. Stir in remaining ingredients. Roll into one-inch balls and place on lightly greased baking sheets; flatten slightly. Bake at 350 degrees for 15 minutes. Makes about 5 dozen.

German Chocolate Delights
Jennifer Holt, Fort Worth, TX

18-1/4 oz. pkg. German chocolate cake mix
1/2 c. oil
2 eggs, beaten
1 single refrigerated chocolate pudding cup
1 c. semi-sweet chocolate chips
1/2 c. long-cooking oats, uncooked
1/2 c. chopped pecans
1 c. sweetened flaked coconut

Combine dry cake mix and remaining ingredients; blend well. Drop dough by rounded teaspoonfuls, 2 inches apart onto ungreased baking sheets. Bake at 350 degrees for 8 to 10 minutes, until set. Cool one minute before removing from baking sheets. Makes about 4-1/2 dozen.

Snickerdoodle Cupcakes
Diana Bulls, Reedley, CA

18-1/4 oz. pkg. white cake mix
1 c. milk
1/2 c. butter, melted and cooled slightly
3 eggs, beaten
1 t. vanilla extract
2 t. cinnamon

In a large bowl, combine dry cake mix and remaining ingredients. Beat with an electric mixer on low speed for 3 minutes. Fill greased muffin tins 2/3 full. Bake at 350 degrees for 22 to 25 minutes. Let cool. Makes one dozen.

Cinnamon Frosting:

1/2 c. butter, softened
1 t. vanilla extract
1 T. cinnamon
3-3/4 c. powdered sugar
3 to 4 T. milk

Beat butter until fluffy. Mix in vanilla, cinnamon and powdered sugar. Stir in enough milk for desired consistency. Frost cupcakes with Cinnamon Frosting.

Quick & Easy Nutty Cheese Bars

Donnie Carter, Wellington, TX

18-1/2 oz. pkg. golden butter cake
  mix
1-1/2 c. chopped pecans or
  walnuts, divided

3/4 c. butter, melted
2 8-oz. pkgs. cream cheese,
  softened
1 c. brown sugar, packed

In a bowl, combine dry cake mix, 3/4 cup pecans and melted butter; stir until well blended. Press mixture into the bottom of a greased 13"x9" baking pan. Combine cream cheese and brown sugar in a separate bowl. Stir until well mixed. Spread evenly over crust. Sprinkle with remaining pecans. Bake at 350 degrees for 25 to 30 minutes, until edges are golden and cheese topping is set. Cool completely in pan on wire rack. Cut into bars. Refrigerate leftovers. Makes 2 dozen.

Just Peachy Blueberry Crisp

Sara Burton, Thornville, OH

3 c. peaches, peeled, pitted and
  sliced
1/2 c. blueberries

2 t. cinnamon-sugar
1 c. all-purpose flour
1 c. brown sugar, packed

1/2 c. butter, softened
3/4 c. long-cooking oats, uncooked

Arrange peaches and blueberries in a buttered 8"x8" baking pan. Sprinkle with cinnamon-sugar; toss gently to coat. In a bowl, combine flour and brown sugar; cut in butter and oats with a fork until mixture is crumbly. Sprinkle mixture evenly over fruit. Bake at 350 degrees for 40 to 45 minutes, until topping is crisp and golden. Serve warm. Serves 6 to 8.

Caramel Fudge Cake

Victoria Alzza, South Amboy, NJ

18-1/4 oz. pkg. chocolate cake mix
1/2 c. butter
14-oz. pkg. caramels, unwrapped

14-oz. can sweetened condensed
  milk

1 c. chopped pecans

Prepare cake according to package directions; pour 2 cups of batter into a greased 13"x9" baking pan. Bake at 350 degrees for 15 minutes; set aside. In a saucepan, melt butter and caramels; remove from heat. Add milk; stir well. Pour over cake; spread remaining cake batter over caramel mixture. Sprinkle with pecans; bake for an additional 30 minutes. Cool before serving. Makes 15 servings.

Just Peachy Blueberry Crisp

Quick tip

Make a handy mixture for greasing and flouring cake pans in one easy step. Combine 1/2 cup shortening with 1/4 cup all-purpose flour. Store in a covered container at room temperature.

Cinnamon-Apple Parfaits

🥄🍴🔪 *Quick tip*

Stock up on cake mixes, pudding mixes and fruit pie fillings whenever they go on sale...mix & match to make all kinds of simply delicious desserts.

Cinnamon-Apple Parfaits

Courtney Robinson, Delaware, OH

1 c. quick-cooking oats, uncooked
1/2 c. brown sugar, packed
1/4 c. butter, melted

21-oz. can apple pie filling,
  warmed
1/4 t. cinnamon

1 qt. vanilla ice cream, slightly
  softened

Combine oats, brown sugar and butter; spread in an ungreased 8"x8" baking pan. Bake at 350 degrees for 10 minutes. Cool; crumble and set aside. Mix together pie filling and cinnamon; divide among 8 parfait glasses. Top with softened ice cream and crumbled oat mixture. Serves 8.

Cookies & Vanilla Cream Fudge

Megan Brooks, Antioch, TN

3 6-oz. pkgs. white chocolate chips
1/8 t. salt

14-oz. can sweetened condensed
  milk

2 c. chocolate sandwich cookies,
  coarsely crushed

Combine chocolate chips, salt and condensed milk in a heavy saucepan over low heat; stir until melted and smooth. Remove from heat; stir in cookies. Spread evenly in a greased aluminum foil-lined 8"x8" baking pan. Chill for 2 hours, or until firm. Turn fudge onto cutting board; peel off foil and cut into squares. Store tightly covered at room temperature. Makes about 3-1/2 dozen.

Triple Fudgy Brownies

Wendy Lee Paffenroth, Pine Island, NY

3.4-oz. pkg. instant chocolate pudding mix

2 c. milk

18-1/2 oz. pkg. chocolate cake mix

Optional: 1 t. vanilla or almond extract

12-oz. pkg. semi-sweet chocolate chips

Optional: powdered sugar

Combine dry pudding mix and milk; stir just until pudding starts to thicken. Stir in dry cake mix and extract, if using. Fold in chocolate chips. Spread batter evenly into a lightly greased 13"x9" baking pan; place on center oven rack. Bake at 350 degrees for about 30 to 40 minutes, until top springs back when lightly touched. Let cool at least one hour before cutting into squares. Dust with powdered sugar, if desired. Makes about 1-1/2 dozen.

Taffy Apple Cupcakes

Angie Biggins, Lyons, IL

18-1/4 oz. pkg. carrot cake mix

1 c. Granny Smith apples, cored, peeled and finely chopped

1/2 t. cinnamon

20 caramels, unwrapped

1/4 c. milk

1 c. pecans or walnuts, finely chopped

12 wooden craft sticks

Prepare cake mix according to package instructions; stir in apples and cinnamon. Fill paper-lined jumbo muffin cups 2/3 full. Bake at 350 degrees for 20 to 25 minutes, until a toothpick inserted near center tests clean. Combine caramels and milk in a small saucepan over low heat; stir until melted and smooth. Drizzle caramel over cooled cupcakes; sprinkle nuts over top. Insert a craft stick into center of each cupcake. Makes one dozen.

Gluten-Free Chocolate Chip Cookies

Joshua Logan, Corpus Christi, TX

3/4 c. butter, softened

1-1/4 c. brown sugar, packed

1/4 c. sugar

1/4 c. egg substitute

1 t. gluten-free vanilla extract

2-1/4 c. gluten-free baking mix

1 t. baking powder

1 t. baking soda

1 t. salt

12-oz. pkg. semi-sweet chocolate chips

Blend together butter and sugars. Gradually stir in egg substitute and vanilla. Sift together remaining ingredients except chocolate chips; add to butter mixture and stir well. Fold in chocolate chips. Drop by teaspoonfuls 2 inches apart onto greased baking sheets. Bake at 375 degrees for 6 to 8 minutes. Cool on baking sheets for 2 minutes; remove to a wire rack to cool completely. Makes 3 dozen.

Triple Fudgy Brownies

Butterscotch Picnic Cake

No-Bake Maple-Peanut Drops

Mary Patenaude, Griswold, CT

1-1/2 c. sugar
1/2 c. milk
1/4 c. maple-flavored syrup
2 t. vanilla extract
1/2 c. creamy peanut butter
2 c. quick-cooking oats, uncooked

Combine sugar, milk and syrup in a medium saucepan; bring to a rolling boil over medium heat, stirring frequently. Boil for 3 minutes; stir in vanilla and peanut butter. Add oats, mixing well. Drop by rounded teaspoonfuls onto wax paper. Cool for 3 to 4 hours, until firm. Makes about 2-1/2 dozen.

Butterscotch Spice Cookies

Kristy Markners, Fort Mill, SC

18-oz. pkg. spice cake mix
2 eggs, beaten
1/2 c. applesauce
1 T. vanilla extract
Optional: 1 c. long-cooking oats, uncooked
11-oz. pkg. butterscotch chips

Combine dry cake mix, eggs, applesauce and vanilla in a large bowl. Add oats, if using. Beat with an electric mixer on low speed until well blended. Stir in butterscotch chips. Drop by rounded teaspoonfuls, 2 inches apart, on parchment paper-lined baking sheets. Bake at 375 degrees for 8 to 10 minutes, until set. Cool cookies for 2 minutes on baking sheets. Remove to wire racks to finish cooling. Makes about 3 dozen.

Butterscotch Picnic Cake

Cindy Neel, Gooseberry Patch

1/2 c. butter
1 c. brown sugar, packed
3 eggs, beaten
1 t. vanilla extract
2 c. all-purpose flour
1 t. baking soda
1 t. salt
1-1/2 c. buttermilk
1 c. quick-cooking oats, uncooked
6-oz. pkg butterscotch chips
1/3 c. chopped walnuts

Beat together butter and brown sugar until light and fluffy. Blend in eggs and vanilla; mix well. Whisk together flour, baking soda and salt. Add flour mixture to butter mixture alternately with buttermilk, mixing well after each addition. Stir in oats. Spread in a greased 13"x9" baking pan. Combine butterscotch chips and nuts; sprinkle over top. Bake at 350 degrees for 30 to 35 minutes. Cool; cut into squares. Serves 15 to 18.

Quick tip

Vintage flowered china plates can be picked up for a song at yard sales. They're just right for delivering cookies to a neighbor or your child's teacher...and there's no need for them to return the plate!

Simple Sweets

Fourth of July Lemon Bars

Marlene Darnell, Newport Beach, CA

16-1/2 oz. pkg. lemon bar mix
1/4 c. powdered sugar
.68-oz. tube red decorating gel
1/4 c. blueberries

Prepare lemon bars as directed on package; bake in an ungreased 9"x9" baking pan. Cool completely in pan on a wire rack. Cut into 6 rectangular bars. Place bars on a serving plate. Sprinkle with powdered sugar. Pipe stripes across bars with decorating gel. Place 6 blueberries in the top corner of each bar. Makes 6.

Red Velvet Bars

Judy Jones, Chinquapin, NC

18-1/2 oz. pkg. red velvet cake mix
2 T. brown sugar, packed
1 t. baking cocoa
2 eggs, beaten
1/2 c. oil
1/2 t. vanilla extract
2 T. water
1 c. white chocolate chips
1/2 c. chopped pecans
Optional: whipped topping, additional chopped pecans

In a large bowl, combine dry cake mix, brown sugar and cocoa. Stir in eggs, oil, vanilla and water. Mix in chocolate chips and pecans. Spray a 13"x9" baking pan with non-stick vegetable spray; spread in batter. Bake at 350 degrees for 18 to 20 minutes. Cool and spread with whipped topping and additional pecans, if using. Cut into bars. Makes 20.

Lemonade Pie

Beverley Williams, San Antonio, TX

14-oz. can sweetened condensed milk
12-oz. can frozen lemonade concentrate, thawed
8-oz. container frozen whipped topping, thawed
2 9-inch graham cracker crusts

In a bowl, mix together condensed milk, lemonade and whipped topping; evenly divide between crusts. Freeze overnight. Makes 2 pies; each serves 6 to 8.

Quick side

Make your own crumb crusts. Combine 1-1/2 cups finely crushed graham crackers or vanilla wafers, 1/4 cup sugar and 1/2 cup melted butter. Mix well and press into a pie plate. Bake at 350 degrees for 10 minutes, cool and fill as desired.

Fourth of July Lemon Bars

Sunny Lemon Blossoms

Classic Cherry Trifle
Howard Cooper, Phoenix, AZ

8-oz. pkg. cream cheese, softened
3/4 c. powdered sugar
1/2 c. milk

1/3 t. vanilla extract
12-oz. container frozen whipped
 topping, thawed

1 angel food cake, cut into cubes
 and divided
2 21-oz. cans cherry pie filling

Blend together cream cheese, sugar, milk and vanilla in a bowl until smooth. Gently fold in whipped topping; set aside. In a large glass bowl, layer half of cake cubes, half of cream cheese mixture and one can pie filling. Repeat layers, ending with pie filling. Cover and refrigerate 3 to 4 hours before serving. Serves 10 to 12.

Sunny Lemon Blossoms
Tina Dillon, Parma, OH

18-1/2 oz. pkg. yellow cake mix
4 eggs, beaten

3.4-oz. pkg. instant lemon
 pudding mix

3/4 c. oil

Combine all ingredients in a large bowl except those for the glaze. Spray mini muffin cups with non-stick vegetable spray; fill cups 1/2 full with batter. Bake at 350 degrees for 12 minutes. Cool in muffin tin on a wire rack 10 minutes; remove cupcakes from tin and cool completely. Dip each cupcake into Lemon Glaze to coat; shake off excess. Place on a wire rack set over a baking sheet; refrigerate until set. Makes 4 dozen.

Lemon Glaze:
4 c. powdered sugar
1/3 c. lemon juice

3 T. lemon zest
3 T. oil

3 T. water

Combine all ingredients; stir until smooth.

Cinnamon Bread Pudding

Sharon Gould, Howard City, MI

6 eggs
2 c. milk
2 c. half-and-half, divided

1 c. sugar
2 t. vanilla extract
6 c. cinnamon bread, cubed

1/2 c. brown sugar, packed
1/4 c. butter
1/2 c. light corn syrup

Beat eggs in a large bowl; whisk in milk, 1-3/4 c. half-and-half, sugar and vanilla. Stir in bread crumb cubes until lightly moistened. Spread mixture evenly in a greased 2-quart casserole dish. Bake at 325 degrees for 55 to 60 minutes, until center starts to firm. In a saucepan over medium-low heat, heat brown sugar and butter until butter melts. Stir in corn syrup and remaining half-and-half. Cook, stirring constantly, until smooth and brown sugar dissolves. Spoon sauce over warm pudding. Serves 8.

Tiramisu Cookie Log

Lori Brooks, Cumming, GA

1 pt. whipping cream
sugar to taste
15-oz. pkg. chocolate chip cookies

2 c. brewed espresso or strong
  coffee, cooled

Garnish: mini semi-sweet
  chocolate chips

Using an electric mixer on medium-high speed, beat together whipping cream and sugar until stiff; set aside. Quickly dip 2 cookies into cooled coffee. Using a dab of whipped cream, sandwich cookies together upright, creating a log. Repeat process until desired length of log is reached. When finished, cover log with remaining whipped cream; garnish with mini chocolate chips. Chill until ready to serve, no more than 3 to 4 hours. Serves about 10.

🥄🍴🔪 *Quick tip*

For a quick dessert garnish, chop nuts and
toast them in a shallow baking pan at
350 degrees for 5 to 10 minutes. Cool, then
place in plastic bags and freeze...ready
to sprinkle on pies, cakes or ice cream
whenever you need them.

Cinnamon Bread Pudding

Quick side

Baked apples are a scrumptious treat. Core apples nearly through and place in a greased casserole dish. Fill each apple with a teaspoon of honey or maple syrup, a teaspoon of butter and a little cinnamon. Bake at 350 degrees for 35 to 45 minutes, until tender. Serve warm, topped with whipped cream,

Fresh Apple Cake

Fresh Apple Cake

Gail Allen, Brownfield, TX

1 c. oil
2 c. sugar
2 eggs, beaten
2-1/2 c. all-purpose flour

1 t. baking soda
1 t. salt
1 t. cinnamon
2 t. vanilla extract

3 c. Golden Delicious apples, cored
  and chopped
1 c. chopped pecans or walnuts
Optional: powdered sugar

Combine oil and sugar in a bowl; add eggs and blend well. In a separate bowl, mix flour, baking soda, salt and cinnamon; add to oil mixture and blend well. Stir in vanilla, apples and nuts. Batter will be very stiff. Spoon into a greased and floured tube pan. Bake at 350 degrees for 50 to 60 minutes. Turn out cake. Sprinkle with powdered sugar, if desired. Serves 16 to 20.

Raisin Spice Cookies

Deborah Moeller, Stockton, IA

18-1/2 oz. pkg. spice cake mix
2 eggs, beaten

1/3 c. oil
3/4 c. raisins

Mix all ingredients together; drop by spoonfuls onto ungreased baking sheets. Bake for 12 to 15 minutes at 350 degrees. Let cool for 5 minutes before removing from baking sheets. Makes 1-1/2 dozen.

Simple Sweets

Apple Crisp Pie

Cris Hamilton, Anna, TX

21-oz. can apple pie filling
9-inch deep-dish pie crust
1/2 c. brown sugar, packed
1/2 c. sugar
1 c. quick-cooking oats, uncooked
1 T. cinnamon
1/4 c. butter, sliced

Pour apple pie filling into pie crust; set aside. In a separate bowl, combine sugars, oats and cinnamon. Sprinkle over top; dot with butter. Bake at 375 degrees for 30 minutes. Serves 8.

Graham No-Bake Cookies

Lisa Langston, Conroe, TX

2 c. sugar
1/2 c. milk
2 T. baking cocoa
1/2 c. butter
1/2 c. creamy peanut butter
1 T. vanilla extract
2 c. quick-cooking oats, uncooked
1 c. graham cracker crumbs

Combine sugar, milk, cocoa and butter in a saucepan over medium heat. Bring to a boil; boil for 2 minutes, stirring constantly. Remove from heat. Stir in peanut butter, vanilla, oats and crumbs; mix well. Drop by rounded tablespoonfuls onto buttered wax paper; cool completely. Makes 4 to 5 dozen.

Chocolate Coconut Bonbons

Melissa Bromen, Marshall, MN

2 1-oz. sqs. unsweetened baking chocolate
14-oz. can sweetened condensed milk
2 c. flaked coconut
1/2 c. chopped walnuts

Melt chocolate in the top of a double boiler over boiling water. Remove from heat and stir in remaining ingredients. Drop by teaspoonfuls onto greased baking sheets, shaping with hands into balls. Preheat oven at 350 degrees; turn off heat. Place baking sheets in oven for 20 minutes or until candies have a glazed appearance. Makes 3 dozen.

Chocolate Coconut Bonbons

Quick side

If you need just a little colored sugar for cookies and cupcakes, make it yourself. Just place 1/4 cup sugar in a small jar, add a drop or two of food coloring, cover the jar and shake to blend well. Spread the sugar on wax paper and let dry.

Grandma's Molasses Crinkles

Grandma's Molasses Crinkles

Linda Leffel, Newark, OH

2 eggs, beaten
1 c. light brown sugar, packed
1 c. dark brown sugar, packed
1-1/2 c. shortening

1/2 c. dark molasses
4-1/2 c. all-purpose flour
3 T. cinnamon
2 t. ground ginger

1 t. ground cloves
4 t. baking soda
1/2 t. salt
Garnish: sugar

Combine eggs, sugars, shortening and molasses in a large bowl. In a separate bowl, sift together remaining ingredients except garnish. Gradually add flour mixture to egg mixture; cover and chill thoroughly. Roll dough into one-inch balls. Dip tops into sugar and place on lightly greased baking sheets, sugar-side up. Press tops down lightly with a fork to flatten. If desired, sprinkle each cookie with a few drops of water for a more crackled surface. Bake at 350 degrees for 10 minutes. Makes 6 to 7 dozen.

Brown Sugar Shortbread Cookies

Renee Velderman, Hopkins, MI

1 c. butter, softened

1/2 c. brown sugar, packed

2-1/4 c. all-purpose flour

Blend together butter and sugar; gradually stir in flour. Turn onto a lightly floured surface and knead until smooth. Pat into an 11"x8" rectangle about 1/3-inch thick; cut into 2-inch by 1-inch strips. Arrange on ungreased baking sheets one inch apart. Pierce surface with a fork. Bake at 300 degrees for 25 minutes, or until beginning to turn golden on bottom. Cool for 5 minutes; remove to a wire rack to cool completely. Makes 3-1/2 dozen.

Gingerbread Brownies

Stephanie Mayer, Portsmouth, VA

1-1/2 c. all-purpose flour
1 c. sugar
1/2 t. baking soda
1/4 c. baking cocoa
1 t. ground ginger

1 t. cinnamon
1/2 t. ground cloves
1/4 c. butter, melted and slightly
  cooled
1/3 c. molasses

2 eggs, beaten
Garnish: powdered sugar

In a large bowl, combine flour, sugar, baking soda, cocoa and spices. In another bowl, combine butter, molasses and eggs. Add butter mixture to flour mixture, stirring until just combined. Spread in a greased 13"x9" baking pan. Bake at 350 degrees for 20 minutes. Cool in pan on a wire rack. Dust with powdered sugar. Cut into squares. Makes 2 dozen.

Buckeye Brownies

Heather Prentice, Mars, PA

19-1/2 oz. pkg. brownie mix
2 c. powdered sugar
8-oz. jar creamy peanut butter

1/2 c. plus 6 T. butter, softened and
  divided

6-oz. pkg. semi-sweet chocolate
  chips

Prepare and bake brownie mix in a greased 13"x9" baking pan according to package directions. Let cool. Mix powdered sugar, peanut butter and 1/2 cup butter. Mix well and spread over cooled brownies. Chill for one hour. Melt together chocolate chips and remaining butter in a saucepan over low heat, stirring occasionally. Spread over brownies. Let cool; cut into squares. Makes 2 to 3 dozen.

Buckeye Brownies

Quick tip

It's easy to save extra whipped cream! Dollop heaping tablespoonfuls onto a chilled baking sheet and freeze. Remove from the baking sheet and store in a plastic zipping bag. To use, place dollops on dessert servings and let stand a few minutes.

Fudge Brownie Pie

Rocky Road Brownies

Sheryl Whited, Austin, TX

19-1/2 oz. pkg. fudge brownie mix
2 c. mini marshmallows, divided
12-oz. pkg. semi-sweet chocolate chips, divided
1 c. dry-roasted peanuts, divided

Prepare brownie mix according to package instructions; spread in a greased 13"x9" baking pan. Sprinkle one cup mini marshmallows, one cup chocolate chips and 1/2 cup peanuts over batter. Bake at 350 degrees for 28 to 30 minutes. Remove from oven; sprinkle with remaining marshmallows, peanuts and chocolate chips. Let cool completely before cutting into squares. Makes 2 to 3 dozen.

Pound Cake S'Mores

Cindy Schmitt, Oelwein, IA

1 pound cake, sliced
1 to 2 c. mini marshmallows
12-oz. pkg. semi-sweet chocolate chips
12-oz. jar caramel ice cream topping
1/2 to 1 c. chopped walnuts

Place cake slices on an ungreased baking sheet; sprinkle with marshmallows and chocolate chips. Place 4 to 6 inches under broiler; broil for 2 to 3 minutes, until marshmallows are lightly golden. Transfer 2 slices each to 6 to 8 serving plates and drizzle with caramel topping; sprinkle with walnuts. Makes 6 to 8 servings.

Fudge Brownie Pie

Flo Burtnett, Gage, OK

1 c. sugar
1/2 c. margarine, melted
2 eggs, beaten
1/2 c. all-purpose flour
1/3 c. baking cocoa
1/4 t. salt
1 t. vanilla extract
1/2 c. chopped walnuts
Garnish: vanilla ice cream

Beat sugar and margarine together. Add eggs; mix well. Stir in flour, cocoa and salt; mix in vanilla and nuts. Pour into a greased and floured 9" pie plate; bake at 350 degrees for 25 to 30 minutes. Cut into wedges; top with scoops of ice cream. Serves 6 to 8.

Simple Sweets

Crustless Pumpkin Pie

Linda Webb, Delaware, OH

4 eggs, beaten
15-oz. can pumpkin
12-oz. can evaporated milk
1-1/2 c. sugar
2 t. pumpkin pie spice
1 t. salt
18-1/2 oz. pkg. yellow cake mix

1 c. chopped pecans or walnuts
1 c. butter, melted
Garnish: whipped topping, chopped nuts, cinnamon

Combine eggs, pumpkin, evaporated milk, sugar, spice and salt. Mix well; pour into an ungreased 13"x9" baking pan. Sprinkle dry cake mix and nuts over top. Drizzle with butter; do not stir. Bake at 350 degrees for 45 minutes to one hour, testing for doneness with a toothpick. Serve with whipped topping, sprinkled with nuts and cinnamon. Makes 8 to 10 servings.

Harvest Fruit & Nut Pie

Angie Venable, Ostrander, OH

4 Granny Smith apples, peeled, cored and sliced
1 c. cranberries
1/2 c. pineapple chunks
1/2 c. chopped walnuts
1 c. sugar
2/3 c. brown sugar, packed

1/4 c. all-purpose flour
1 t. cinnamon
1/4 t. nutmeg
4 9-inch deep-dish pie crusts
3 T. butter

Mix together apples, cranberries, pineapple, walnuts and sugar. Sift together brown sugar, flour, cinnamon and nutmeg; add to apple mixture. Arrange 2 pie crusts in two 9" pie plates. Divide mixture equally between pie crusts; dot each with butter and cover with top pie crust, crimping to seal. Bake at 400 degrees for 45 minutes. Makes 2 pies; each serves 6.

Blue-Ribbon Pecan Pie

Suzy Grubich, Eighty Four, PA

9-inch pie crust, unbaked
1/2 c. pecan halves
3 eggs
1 c. dark corn syrup

1 c. sugar
1 t. vanilla extract
1/8 t. salt

Place unbaked crust in a 9" pie plate. Arrange pecans in crust; set aside. In a bowl, beat eggs well. Add remaining ingredients; mix well. Pour mixture over pecans in crust. Bake at 400 degrees for 15 minutes; reduce oven to 325 degrees. Bake an additional 30 minutes, or until center of pie is set. Cool completely. Serves 8.

Quick tip

For an affordable get-together, invite friends over for "just desserts!" Offer 2 to 3 simple homebaked desserts like cobblers, dump cake and fruit pie, ice cream for topping and a steamy pot of coffee...they'll love it!

Crustless Pumpkin Pie

Mini Mousse Cupcakes

Mini Mousse Cupcakes
Vickie

2-1/3 c. milk chocolate
  chips
6 eggs, beaten
1/4 c. plus 2 T. all-purpose
  flour

Garnish: whipped cream,
  chocolate shavings

Melt chocolate chips in a double boiler over medium heat and let cool slightly. In a large bowl, beat eggs and flour. Beat in melted chocolate until combined. Fill paper-lined mini muffin cups 2/3 full. Bake at 325 degrees for 7 to 10 minutes, until edges are done and centers shake slightly. Cool in tin on wire rack for 20 minutes. Remove from tin; cool completely. Garnish with whipped cream and chocolate shavings. Makes about 2 dozen.

Eclair Cake
Cheryl Frost, Woodstock, OH

1 c. water
1/2 c. butter
1 c. all-purpose flour
4 eggs, beaten
8-oz. pkg. cream cheese,
  softened

3 c. milk
2 3-oz. pkgs. instant
  vanilla pudding mix
8-oz. container frozen
  whipped topping, thawed
Garnish: chocolate syrup

Combine water and butter in a saucepan; heat until boiling. Whisk in flour until smooth; remove from heat. Pour mixture into a medium bowl; gradually blend in eggs. Spread in a greased 13"x9" baking pan; bake at 350 degrees for 30 minutes. Remove from oven; press baked crust down lightly and set aside. With an electric mixer on medium speed, beat together cream cheese, milk and pudding mix for 2 minutes; spread over crust. Refrigerate until firm. At serving time, spread with whipped topping; drizzle with chocolate syrup. Serves 12 to 15.

Banana Supreme Pie
Regina Kostyu, Columbus, OH

3.4-oz. pkg. instant vanilla
  pudding mix
1 c. sour cream
1/2 c. milk
12-oz. container frozen
  whipped topping, thawed

1 to 2 ripe bananas, sliced
9-inch graham cracker
  crust

Stir together pudding mix, sour cream, milk and whipped topping; set aside. Arrange banana slices in bottom of pie crust. Spoon pudding mixture over bananas; chill until serving time. Makes 6 servings.

Quick tip

Baking together is a fun family activity and a great choice for kids just starting to learn how to cook. As you measure, mix and bake together, be sure to share any stories about hand-me-down cake or cookie recipes... you'll be creating memories as well as sweet treats!

Root Beer Float Cake

Mary Patenaude, Griswold, CT

18-1/2 oz. pkg. white cake mix
2-1/4 c. root beer, chilled and
   divided

1/4 c. oil
2 eggs, beaten

1 env. whipped topping mix

In a large bowl, combine dry cake mix, 1-1/4 cups root beer, oil and eggs; beat until well blended. Pour into a greased 13"x9" baking pan. Bake at 350 degrees for 30 to 35 minutes; cool completely. In a medium bowl, with an electric mixer on high speed, beat whipped topping mix and remaining root beer until soft peaks form; frost cake. Makes 24 servings.

My Mom's Muffin Donuts

Laura Parker, Flagstaff, AZ

2 c. all-purpose flour
1/2 t. salt
1 T. baking powder
1/2 t. nutmeg

1/2 c. plus 1/2 t. butter, divided
1-1/2 c. sugar, divided
1 egg, beaten
3/4 c. milk

3/4 c. semi-sweet chocolate chips
1/2 c. chopped pecans
2 t. cinnamon

Combine flour, salt, baking powder, nutmeg, 1/2 teaspoon butter, 1/2 cup sugar, egg and milk. Fold in chocolate chips and pecans. Fill greased muffin cups 2/3 full. Bake at 350 degrees for 20 minutes. Remove immediately from pan. Melt the remaining butter; roll muffins in butter. Combine remaining sugar and cinnamon; roll muffins in mixture. Makes one dozen.

My Mom's Muffin Donuts

Strawberry Layer Cake

Aunt Marge's Peachy Pineapple Dessert

Marilyn Just, DeSoto, KS

20-oz. can crushed
  pineapple
29-oz. can sliced peaches
18-1/2-oz. pkg. white or
  yellow cake mix
1/2 to 1 c. chopped walnuts
  or pecans
3/4 to 1 c. butter, melted

In an ungreased 13"x9" glass baking pan, evenly spread pineapple with juices; add peaches with juices. Sprinkle with dry cake mix, then with nuts. Drizzle with melted butter; do not stir. Bake at 350 degrees for 35 to 40 minutes, until bubbly and top is lightly golden. Serve warm. Serves 10 to 12.

Mandarin Orange Cake

Nancy Likens, Wooster, OH

18-1/2 oz. pkg. white cake
  mix
11-oz. can mandarin
  oranges, drained and
  juice reserved
3 egg whites
1/2 c. oil
2 8-oz. cans crushed
  pineapple
3-1/2 oz. pkg. instant
  vanilla pudding mix
8-oz. container frozen
  whipped topping, thawed
1 c. sweetened flaked
  coconut, divided

Combine dry cake mix, reserved orange juice, egg whites and oil. Beat with an electric mixer on medium speed for 2 minutes, until creamy. Fold in oranges; pour into a greased and floured 13"x9" baking pan. Bake at 350 degrees for 25 to 35 minutes, until a toothpick in the center comes out clean. Place pan on a wire rack to cool completely. Pour pineapple and its juice into a medium bowl; stir in dry pudding mix. Fold in whipped topping and 1/2 cup coconut. Mix well; chill while cake is cooling. Spread over top and sides; sprinkle with remaining coconut. Serve immediately or keep refrigerated. Serves 12.

Strawberry Layer Cake

Steven Wilson, Chesterfield, VA

6-oz. pkg. strawberry
  gelatin mix
1/2 c. hot water
18-1/2 oz. pkg. white cake
  mix
2 T. all-purpose flour
1 c. strawberries, hulled
  and chopped
4 eggs

In a large bowl, dissolve dry gelatin mix in hot water; cool. Add dry cake mix, flour and strawberries; mix well. Add eggs, one at a time, beating slightly after each one. Pour batter into 3 greased 8" round cake pans. Bake at 350 degrees for 20 minutes, or until cake tests done with a toothpick. Cool; assemble layers with Strawberry Frosting. Serves 12.

Strawberry Frosting:

1/4 c. butter, softened
3-3/4 to 5 c. powdered
  sugar
1/3 c. strawberries, hulled
  and finely chopped

Blend butter and powdered sugar together, adding sugar to desired consistency. Add strawberries; blend thoroughly.

Quick side

Turn canned fruit into cool fruit sorbet...it's easy! Freeze an unopened can of apricots, peaches or another favorite fruit. At serving time, open the can, scoop out the frozen fruit and process it in a food processor until smooth.

INDEX

INDEX

INDEX

INDEX

Salads

Sandwiches

Sides

Snacks

Soups & Stews

Send us your favorite recipe

...and the memory that makes it special for you!

If we select your recipe for a brand-new **Gooseberry Patch** cookbook, your name will appear right along with it...and you'll receive a FREE copy of the book!

**Submit your recipe on our website at
www.gooseberrypatch.com/sharearecipe or mail to:
Gooseberry Patch, PO Box 812, Columbus, OH 43216**

*Please include the number of servings and all other necessary information.

Have a taste for more?

Visit www.gooseberrypatch.com to join our Circle of Friends!

- Free recipes, tips and ideas plus a complete cookbook index
- Get special email offers and our monthly eLetter delivered to your inbox